SO-DZN-570

Antioch Community High School
Library

621

Antioch Community High School
Library
1133 S. Main Street
Antioch, IL 60002

DEMCO

ARBITRARY BORDERS

Political Boundaries in World History

The Division of the Middle East
The Treaty of Sèvres

Northern Ireland and England
The Troubles

The Great Wall of China

The Green Line
The Division of Palestine

The Iron Curtain
The Cold War in Europe

The Mason–Dixon Line

Vietnam: The 17th Parallel

Korea Divided: The 38th Parallel and the Demilitarized Zone

The U.S.–Mexico Border
The Treaty of Guadalupe Hidalgo

The Czech Republic: The Velvet Revolution

Louisiana Territory

South Africa: A State of Apartheid

The Partition of British India

London: From the Walled City to New Towns

A South American Frontier: The Tri-Border Region

China Contested: Western Powers in East Asia

The Breakup of Yugoslavia: Conflict in the Balkans

The Dispute Over Gibraltar

Balkan Peninsula, 2001

SLOVAKIA UKRAINE

AUSTRIA MOLDOVA

HUNGARY

Mures R.

Ljubljana
Zagreb
SLOVENIA ROMANIA
Sava R. CROATIA VOJVODINA
Vinkovci Novi Sad
Belgrade
Banja Luka Bucharest
Srebrenica
YUGOSLAVIA SERBIA
BOSNIA-
HERZEGOVINA Sarajevo
Split Danube R.
Leskovac Black
Adriatic Sea Podgorica Pristina Sea
MONTENEGRO KOSOVO Sofia BULGARIA

ITALY Skopje

Tirana MACEDONIA*

ALBANIA Sea of
Marmara

Corfu GREECE Aegean
(GREECE) Sea

Ionian Sea Rhodes
(GREECE)
Athens

Serbian Republic

Federation of Bosnia
and Herzegovina

Autonomous province
borders

Mediterranean Sea

0   150 miles
Crete
0   150 km (GREECE)

N

* Former Yugoslav Republic
of Macedonia

© Infobase Publishing

ARBITRARY BORDERS

Political Boundaries in World History

The Breakup of Yugoslavia: Conflict in the Balkans

Kate Transchel
California State University, Chico

Foreword by
Senator **George J. Mitchell**

Introduction by
James I. Matray
California State University, Chico

CHELSEA HOUSE
P U B L I S H E R S
An imprint of Infobase Publishing

Frontis By 2001, the country known as Yugoslavia, or "land of the South Slavs," had been officially dissolved. Depicted here are the republics that once made up Yugoslavia—Bosnia and Herzegovina, Croatia, Macedonia, Montenegro, Serbia, and Slovenia—along with the other countries of the Balkan Peninsula.

The Breakup of Yugoslavia: Conflict in the Balkans

Copyright © 2007 by Infobase Publishing

All rights reserved. No part of this book may be reproduced or utilized in any form or by any means, electronic or mechanical, including photocopying, recording, or by any information storage or retrieval systems, without permission in writing from the publisher. For information contact:

Chelsea House
An imprint of Infobase Publishing
132 West 31st Street
New York NY 10001

Library of Congress Cataloging-in-Publication Data

Transschel, Kate.
   The breakup of Yugoslavia : conflict in the Balkans / Kate Transchel.
     p. cm. — (Arbitrary borders)
   Includes bibliographical references and index.
   ISBN 0-7910-8651-8 (hardcover)
   1. Yugoslav War, 1991-1995. 2. Yugoslavia—History.   I. Title.
   DR1313T73 2006
   949.703—dc22   2006019746

Chelsea House books are available at special discounts when purchased in bulk quantities for businesses, associations, institutions, or sales promotions. Please call our Special Sales Department in New York at (212) 967–8800 or (800) 322–8755.

You can find Chelsea House on the World Wide Web at
http://www.chelseahouse.com

Text and cover design by Takeshi Takahashi

Printed in the United States of America

Bang EJB 10 9 8 7 6 5 4 3 2 1

This book is printed on acid-free paper.

All links and Web addresses were checked and verified to be correct at the time of publication. Because of the dynamic nature of the Web, some addresses and links may have changed since publication and may no longer be valid.

Contents

Foreword

Senator **George J. Mitchell**

I spent years working for peace in Northern Ireland and in the Middle East. I also made many visits to the Balkans during the long and violent conflict there.

Each of the three areas is unique; so is each conflict. But there are also some similarities: in each, there are differences over religion, national identity, and territory.

Deep religious differences that lead to murderous hostility are common in human history. Competing aspirations involving national identity are more recent occurrences, but often have been just as deadly.

Territorial disputes—two or more people claiming the same land—are as old as humankind. Almost without exception, such disputes have been a factor in recent conflicts. It is impossible to calculate the extent to which the demand for land—as opposed to religion, national identity, or other factors—figures in the motivation of people caught up in conflict. In my experience it is a substantial factor that has played a role in each of the three conflicts mentioned above.

In Northern Ireland and the Middle East, the location of the border was a major factor in igniting and sustaining the conflict. And it is memorialized in a dramatic and visible way: through the construction of large walls whose purpose is to physically separate the two communities.

In Belfast, the capital and largest city in Northern Ireland, the so-called "Peace Line" cuts through the heart of the city, right across urban streets. Up to thirty feet high in places, topped with barbed wire in others, it is an ugly reminder of the duration and intensity of the conflict.

In the Middle East, as I write these words, the government of Israel has embarked on a huge and controversial effort to construct a security fence roughly along the line that separates Israel from the West Bank.

Having served a tour of duty with the U.S. Army in Berlin, which was once the site of the best known of modern walls, I am skeptical of their long-term value, although they often serve short-term needs. But it cannot be said that such structures represent a new idea. Ancient China built the Great Wall to deter nomadic Mongol tribes from attacking its population.

In much the same way, other early societies established boundaries and fortified them militarily to achieve the goal of self-protection. Borders always have separated people. Indeed, that is their purpose.

This series of books examines the important and timely issue of the significance of arbitrary borders in history. Each volume focuses attention on a territorial division, but the analytical approach is more comprehensive. These studies describe arbitrary borders as places where people interact differently from the way they would if the boundary did not exist. This pattern is especially pronounced where there is no geographic reason for the boundary and no history recognizing its legitimacy. Even though many borders have been defined without legal precision, governments frequently have provided vigorous monitoring and military defense for them.

This series will show how the migration of people and exchange of goods almost always work to undermine the separation that borders seek to maintain. The continuing evolution of a European community provides a contemporary example illustrating this point, most obviously with the adoption of a single currency. Moreover, even former Soviet bloc nations have eliminated barriers to economic and political integration.

Globalization has emerged as one of the most powerful forces in international affairs during the twenty-first century. Not only have markets for the exchange of goods and services become genuinely worldwide, but instant communication and sharing of information have shattered old barriers separating people. Some scholars even argue that globalization has made the entire concept of a territorial nation-state irrelevant. Although the assertion is certainly premature and probably wrong, it highlights the importance of recognizing how borders often have reflected and affirmed the cultural, ethnic, or linguistic perimeters that define a people or a country.

Since the Cold War ended, competition over resources or a variety of interests threaten boundaries more than ever, resulting in contentious interaction, conflict, adaptation, and intermixture. How people define their borders is also a factor in determining how events develop in the surrounding region. This series will provide detailed descriptions of selected arbitrary borders in history with the objective of providing insights on how artificial boundaries separating people will influence international affairs during the next century.

Senator George J. Mitchell

September 2005

Introduction

James I. Matray
California State University, Chico

Throughout history, borders have separated people. Scholars have devoted considerable attention to assessing the significance and impact of territorial boundaries on the course of human history, explaining how they often have been sources of controversy and conflict. In the modern age, the rise of nation-states in Europe created the need for governments to negotiate treaties to confirm boundary lines that periodically changed as a consequence of wars and revolutions. European expansion in the nineteenth century imposed new borders on Africa and Asia. Many native peoples viewed these boundaries as arbitrary and, after independence, continued to contest their legitimacy. At the end of both world wars in the twentieth century, world leaders drew artificial and impermanent lines separating assorted people around the globe. Borders certainly are among the most important factors that have influenced the development of world affairs.

Chelsea House Publishers decided to publish a collection of books looking at arbitrary borders in history in response to the revival of the nuclear crisis in North Korea in October 2002. Recent tensions on the Korean peninsula are a direct consequence of Korea's partition at the 38th parallel at the end of World War II. Other nations in human history have suffered because of similar artificial divisions that have been the result of either international or domestic factors and often a combination of both. In the case of Korea, the United States and the Soviet Union decided in August 1945 to divide the country into two zones of military occupation ostensibly to facilitate the surrender of Japanese forces. However, a political contest was then underway inside Korea to determine the future of the nation after forty years of Japanese colonial rule. The Cold War then created two Koreas with sharply contrasting political, social, and economic systems that symbolized an ideological split among the Korean people. Borders separate people, but rarely prevent their economic, political, social, and cultural interaction. But in Korea, an artificial border has existed since 1945 as a nearly impenetrable barrier precluding meaningful contact between two portions of the same population. Ultimately, two authentic Koreas emerged, exposing how an arbitrary boundary can create circumstances resulting even in the permanent division of a homogeneous people in a historically united land.

Korea's experience in dealing with artificial division may well be unique, but it is not without historical parallels. The first group of books in this series on arbitrary boundaries provided description and analysis of the division of the Middle East after World War I, the Iron Curtain in Central Europe during the Cold War, the United States-Mexico Border, the 17th parallel in Vietnam, and the Mason-Dixon Line. Three authors in a second set of studies addressed the Great Wall in China, the Green Line in Israel, and the 38th parallel and demilitarized zone in Korea. Four other volumes described how discord over artificial borders in the Louisiana Territory, Northern Ireland, Czechoslovakia, and South Africa provide insights about fundamental disputes focusing on sovereignty, religion, and ethnicity. Six books now complete the series. Three authors explore the role of arbitrary boundaries in shaping the history of the city of London, the partition of British India, and the Tri-Border Region in Latin America. Finally, there are studies examining Britain's dispute with Spain over Gibraltar, Modern China, and the splintering of Yugoslavia after the end of the Cold War.

Admittedly, there are many significant differences between these boundaries, but these books will strive to cover as many common themes as possible. In so doing, each will help readers conceptualize how complex factors such as colonialism, culture, and economics determine the nature of contact between people along these borders. Although globalization has emerged as a powerful force working against the creation and maintenance of lines separating people, boundaries likely will endure as factors having a persistent influence on world events. This series of books will provide insights about the impact of arbitrary borders on human history and how such borders continue to shape the modern world.

James I. Matray
Chico, California
September 2005

1

War Comes
to Yugoslavia

In early September 1991, 11-year-old Zlata Filipovic looked forward to school starting again with happy anticipation. Zlata was like millions of 11-year-old girls the world over, and now she was back home in Sarajevo, Bosnia, after spending a summer at the beach, with friends. She thought only of pop music, movies, boys, skiing in the mountains near Sarajevo, and going to the beach. Her family was comfortably well off and she was surrounded by loving neighbors, relatives, and friends. The first entry in her diary on Monday, September 2, 1991, gives no hint of the crisis about to overtake her and all of Sarajevo:

> Behind me—a long hot summer and the happy days of summer holidays; ahead of me—a new school year. I'm starting fifth grade. I'm looking forward to seeing my friends at school and being together again. . . . I'm glad we'll be together again, and share all the worries and joys of going to school.[1]

Little did she know that within a few months her world would be torn apart by war. Some of those very friends she mentioned in her journal would be killed while playing in a park.

The Serbian Army set up artillery positions in the hills directly behind Zlata's apartment building. It shelled Sarajevo from that location for nearly four years. Zlata and her family had to move all their possessions into the front room of their elegant apartment, while they lived barricaded behind sandbags to escape being hit by shrapnel. In no time, the impact of the shells shattered all the apartment's windows. Indeed, before the end of the year, the shelling damaged or destroyed every building in Sarajevo. No one was safe from attack.

Hundreds of Bosnians fled, but others, unable to imagine that their city would be reduced to rubble, refused to leave. Many of Zlata's friends and relatives escaped Sarajevo, leaving Zlata despairing of ever seeing them again. Eventually, the Serbs blockaded all roads leading into and out of Sarajevo and shut down the airport. About 400,000 residents were trapped in the siege. Thousands of civilians were killed or wounded, and every imaginable offense against human rights, from ethnic cleansing (expulsion, imprisonment, or killing of ethnic minorities) and rape to mass executions and starvation, was committed.

While heavy artillery pounded Sarajevo, Zlata and her family spent day after dreary day huddled in a neighbor's basement. Supplies became scarce and then disappeared altogether. Residents came very close to complete starvation. Their only chance for survival depended on food from United Nations (UN) airlifts. The city had no medical supplies, no electricity, no phone service, and no running water. Zlata, therefore, could not watch television, listen to the radio, bathe, or even flush the toilet. Because Serbs often targeted schools and playgrounds, school was suspended, and it became too dangerous for Zlata to play outside. Even standing in line for bread or water meant risking one's life.

Less than a year after her first diary entry, on Monday, June 29, 1992, Zlata came to understand that nothing in her life would ever be the same again:

BOREDOM!!! SHOOTING!!! SHELLING!!! PEOPLE BEING KILLED!!! DESPAIR!!! HUNGER!!! MISERY!!! FEAR!!! That's my life! The life of an innocent 11-year-old school girl. A schoolgirl without a school, without the fun and excitement of school. A child without games, without friends, without the sun, without birds, without nature, without fruit, without chocolate or sweets, with just a little powdered milk. In short, a child without a childhood. A wartime child. I realize now that I am living through a war, I am witnessing an ugly, disgusting, war. I and thousands of other children in this town that is being destroyed, that is crying, weeping, seeking help, but getting none. God, will this ever stop, will I ever be a schoolgirl again, will I ever enjoy my childhood again? I once heard that childhood is the most wonderful time of your life. And it is. I loved it, and now an ugly war is taking it all away from me. Why? I feel sad. I feel like crying. I am crying.[2]

Like millions of people living in Yugoslavia, Zlata was the victim of forces larger than herself. She was nearly crushed by issues she could not comprehend: ethnic cleansing, nationalistic hatreds, and the reworking of arbitrary borders. After nearly a year of constant warfare, Zlata describes in her diary on Tuesday, May 4, 1993, the tragic senselessness of all the killing and destruction:

> I've been thinking about politics again. No matter how stupid, ugly, and unreasonable I think this division of people into Serbs, Croats, and Muslims is, the stupid politics are making it happen. We're all waiting for something, hoping for something, but there's nothing. Even the Vance-Owen peace plan looks as though it's going to fall through [the first failed peace plan]. Now these maps are being drawn up, separating people, and nobody asks them a thing. Those "kids" [Zlata's term for politicians] really are playing around with us. Ordinary people don't want this division because it won't make anybody happy—not the Serbs, not the Croats, not the Muslims.[3]

The Serbian attack on Bosnia in which Zlata was hopelessly trapped was the result of the breakup of Yugoslavia and the random redrawing of already arbitrary borders. Yugoslavia, which literally means the "land of the South Slavs," was a nation artificially created from the ashes of World War I. It consisted of the mostly Catholic regions of Slovenia and Croatia, with Eastern Orthodox Serbia and Montenegro. It also included Bosnia, a land ethnically and religiously divided among Catholic Croats, Orthodox Serbs, and Muslim Slavs. These divisions, created and hardened over centuries, were the real enemies that victimized Zlata and hundreds of thousands like her.

Many troubles plagued Yugoslavia long before it broke apart. Foreign debt, inflation, and unemployment had created tensions within the country as early as 1990. Strong nationalist feelings and political oppositions were even more problematic

Slobodan Milošević, pictured here in 1991, became president of Serbia in 1987 and Yugoslavia in 1997. The former Communist bureaucrat quickly gained the support of his countrymen by inciting Serb nationalism and using his control of the media, police, and the military to stir up hatred toward other ethnicities within the former Yugoslavia.

and eroded the cohesion of Yugoslavia. Consisting of several ethnically diverse republics, Yugoslavia managed to remain a viable state until the 1990s primarily because of centralized Communist rule. With the failure of Communist governments to retain control throughout central and eastern Europe following the fall of the Berlin Wall in 1989, old nationalist antagonisms began to surface. In the early 1990s, the Serbian politician Slobodan Milošević gained popularity in Yugoslavia by inciting Serb nationalism.

These nationalistic antagonisms resulted from tensions festering along arbitrary religious, social, and national borders that developed over centuries. All the peoples of Yugoslavia originally came from the same Slavic tribes that settled on the Balkan Peninsula in the sixth and seventh centuries A.D. Because of the caprice of imperial control—the influence of both the Orthodox and Catholic churches, and different historical experiences—

THE 1974 YUGOSLAV CONSTITUTION

The political disintegration of Yugoslavia and its descent into war to redraw arbitrary political borders had numerous origins. Perhaps one of the more important sources of nationalistic divisions can be found in the 1974 Yugoslav Constitution. In 1974, the Yugoslav government adopted a new constitution—the world's longest, with 406 original articles—which lasted until the end of the 1980s. By giving greater powers to the republics and the provinces of Kosovo and Vojvodina, this new constitution eroded the unifying power of the federal government and allowed the rise of nationalist interests to take precedence over national interests.

The new constitution strengthened the power of the then-President Josip Broz Tito. It also enhanced the political role of the Yugoslav People's Army (JNA) by making it the ninth member of the collective presidency of the Yugoslav Communist Party—the other eight members being the six republics (Serbia, Croatia, Slovenia, Macedonia, Bosnia, and Herzegovina) and the two provinces. According to the constitution, all the republics and provinces were represented equally in federal organs. Republics and provinces could develop their own independent foreign relations, and they were responsible for the organization of territorial defense. In short, sovereignty rested with the republics and the provinces, and not with the federal government. The reaction to these constitutional provisions was an increase in Serbian nationalism. Serb hard-liners believed the constitutional provisions undermined Serbia's territorial borders by giving "sovereignty" to its two provinces, Kosovo and Vojvodina.

over time these tribes adopted differing national identities. Speaking the same language, having similar physical attributes, and sharing a common culture was not sufficient to unite these people in the face of overwhelming religious, social, and nationalistic differences. When nationalism turned to hate, the differences among these groups turned deadly.

In March and April 1990, the Yugoslav republics of Slovenia and Croatia held their first multiparty elections in nearly 50 years. The Communist reformers lost to parties favoring national independence within a loose federation of Yugoslav

According to the constitution, every question had to be agreed upon and approved by the country's eight national states (six republics and two provinces). This meant that every question had to be cleared in one's own state and then returned for final agreement at the federal level. This complicated process "nationalized" each question and strengthened Yugoslavia's arbitrary ethnic and national borders.

Each year, the position of president of Yugoslavia would rotate among representatives of the eight national states. In reality, however, the country was controlled by Tito and the JNA. As long as Tito was alive, this system worked relatively well. Tito's aim in adopting this constitution was to provide a system that would survive his death. In this regard, he aimed to offset the power of the Serb majority by replacing the principle of "one man, one vote" with "one republic, one vote."

When Tito died in 1980, Yugoslavia's collective presidency assumed full control, as stipulated in the 1974 constitution. Most Yugoslavs genuinely mourned the loss of their leader, who had been the country's strongest unifying force. Unfortunately, following Tito's death, the country's political elites began a competition for real power. In a country where historical, social, cultural, and political borders fostered division more than unity, those leaders who appealed to nationalistic objectives quickly gained popularity. What resulted was the dismemberment of Yugoslavia, as well as wars to strengthen and extend arbitrary borders.

states. Later in the year, similar parties won elections in the republics of Macedonia and Bosnia-Herzegovina. The presidents of those countries sought a democratic way to keep Yugoslavia a decentralized and reorganized union of states. Both men feared that if Slovenia and Croatia gained independence from the Yugoslav federation, Bosnia and Macedonia would be swallowed up by the growing nationalism of Serbian President Slobodan Milošević.

Their fears soon came true. According to the Yugoslav Constitution, each year a different Yugoslav state chose the president of the Yugoslav federation. In 1991, it was Croatia's turn at the federal presidency. They selected Stipe Mesić, a non-Communist moderate. Communist Serb leaders blocked the election, however. The Croats, authorized by the Croatian parliament (called the *Sabor*), responded by declaring their independence on the evening of June 25, 1991. Earlier that day, Slovenia had declared independence from what it saw as a nation dominated by Serbs.

Unlike the Croats, the Slovenes had prepared well for independence. They had already created and staffed independent bodies that, on June 26, took control of the borders, air traffic, and the port authorities. At all the borders with neighboring countries, they replaced Yugoslav symbols, flags, and billboards with the emblems of the new independent Republic of Slovenia. They also ordered all federal (that is, Yugoslav) police and customs officials out of Slovenia. By creating their own artificial borders, the Slovenes hoped to make a successful transition to independence from Yugoslavia.

The federal Yugoslav People's Army (JNA) attempted to prevent the breakaway republics from leaving the Yugoslav federation. Wars ensued. Slovenia's war in 1991 against the Serb-dominated JNA lasted only 10 days. Because of American and European pressure, Serbian President Milošević withdrew JNA troops from Slovenia. Milošević also backed the formal recognition of Slovenia's right to peaceful succession. Consequently, the secession of Slovenia from Yugoslavia was formalized on

July 8, 1991. Within three months, Macedonia declared independence with no resistance from the JNA.

Slovenia's war of independence was relatively benign, because it fought against a federal Yugoslavia that was already weakened under growing Serb nationalism. The two wars that followed were much more motivated by nationalism—between Orthodox Serbs and Catholic Croats, and Serbs and Muslim Bosnians. Unable to defend Yugoslavia's territorial integrity, the JNA, defeated and humiliated, withdrew from Slovenia. Within three months, however, the JNA mobilized tens of thousands of Serbs to fight an undeclared war in Croatia. The JNA thus became the Army of Serbs, fighting to extend Serbian territory outside Serbia. It aimed to occupy and annex large areas of Croatia.

Croatia's war with the Serb-dominated Yugoslav Army lasted longer and created more devastation than the 10-day conflict in Slovenia. In the spring of 1991, guerrilla fighters, aided by President Milošević and Serb leaders, invaded every Serb majority district or village in Croatia and armed villagers, who then violently invaded non-Serb-majority districts and villages. In some areas, Serb militias rounded up entire populations of Croats. Those not slaughtered were shipped out of the area. The Serbs killed or displaced thousands.

By the end of the year, Croatia won its independence from Yugoslavia, but at a terrible price. Yugoslavia redrew its borders, partitioned Croatia into Serb and Croat regions, and eventually annexed Serb-populated territories of Croatia. In short, the war created arbitrary borders that left one-third of the country under Serb occupation and cut Croatia almost in half.

When the European Community (EC) and the United States formally recognized Croatia as an independent state in January 1992, it placed Bosnia's president Alija Izetbegović "between a rock and a hard place." He could either seek independence for Bosnia or remain in Serb-dominated Yugoslavia. The EC and the United States encouraged him to declare independence.

The Serbs who lived in this ethnically diverse area, however, feared being controlled by the Muslim Slavs who formed the majority of the population of Bosnia. Radovan Karadžić, the leader of the Bosnian Serbs, threatened that if Bosnia was recognized as an independent state, it would be "stillborn and not survive a single day."[4] Despite his threats, in March 1992, Bosnia-Herzegovina declared its independence from the Yugoslav federation. The Serbs responded by arming themselves and waging war. In less than a month, most of the towns in Bosnia-Herzegovina, except Sarajevo, fell to the Serbs.

Until April 5, 1992, like Zlata, most of Sarajevo's citizens— Muslims, Serbs, Croats, Yugoslavs, and Jews—believed that war would never come to their city. They viewed Karadžić's threats as the ravings of a nationalistic fanatic. Yet, on April 6, they began to take him seriously. On that day, the EC formally recognized Bosnia's independence. Also on that day, Serb militants opened fire on thousands of peace demonstrators in Sarajevo, killing at least 5 and wounding 30. Thus began the siege that destroyed Zlata's childhood.

Recognition of the independence of Macedonia, Croatia, Slovenia, and Bosnia by the EC and the United States posed a problem for Yugoslavia. It was fast becoming a federation with no republics. Shortly after the siege of Sarajevo began, on April 27, 1992, the republics of Serbia and Montenegro joined to proclaim a new Federal Republic of Yugoslavia, with Milošević as president. This new federation marked the end of the Yugoslavia that had been created after World War I.

Independence brought terrible suffering to Bosnia's Muslims. In the spring and summer of 1992, Serb paramilitary hit squads systematically swept through Muslim areas of Bosnia, seizing control of the region without encountering much military resistance. By the end of April 1992, 286,000 refugees had fled Bosnia into Croatia. By early June, this figure rose to 750,000, and by mid-July more than 1.1 million refugees poured out of Bosnia. By the end of the year, 1.5 million Bosnians, nearly half the population, had lost their homes.[5]

The Bosnian refugees brought with them stories that the world at first did not want to believe: tales of torture, mass killings and deportations, the wholesale burning of towns and villages, and sadistic cruelty so horrific that they were accused of lying to discredit their enemy. These people were the victims of ethnic cleansing perpetrated by the Serbs. The goal was to render a territory ethnically pure—in other words free of Muslims and Catholics, so that only Serbs remained. The Serbs intended to instill such hatred and fear that Muslims and Serbs never could live together again.

The Serb paramilitary squads used humiliation, terror, and mental cruelty on a level not seen in Europe since the Nazi death camps of World War II. Men captured by the Serbs were told that their wives had been raped and killed, that their children were dead. The Serbs forced Muslim prisoners upon the threat of death to perform atrocities against each other—mutilations, physical and sexual torture, and even mutual killing. Prisoners were forced to dig mass graves and collect and bury the bodies of their families and friends. Serbs rounded up thousands of men and women into concentration camps, where they were beaten, raped, starved, and ultimately left to die.

The fighting continued into 1994. Help finally came through the intervention of the United Nations, NATO, the EC, and the United States, largely because Sarajevo's plight caught the attention of the Western media. Western television crews, alongside UN peace monitors, watched helplessly as the Serbs shelled the remaining inhabitants of this once-cosmopolitan city that had united in multiethnic demonstrations of solidarity against ethnic hatreds. After an explosion in a market on February 5, 1994, killed 69 people and injured hundreds more, NATO stepped in to protect what remained of Sarajevo.

Zlata was not there to witness the final destruction of her beloved city. On December 23, 1993, two French armored vehicles took Zlata and her parents through government and Serb checkpoints to the airport. A few hours later, they left aboard a UN airplane for the safety of Paris.

One can only imagine Zlata's joy when she heard of the cease-fire that was reached on February 23, 1994. The following

During the Yugoslav Wars of the early 1990s, the Serbian paramilitary terrorized thousands of Bosnians and forced thousands more to flee to Croatia. Pictured here are prisoners at the Manjača detention camp in northern Bosnia and Herzegovina, where detainees were often tortured and killed.

month, Muslims and Croats signed an accord and formed a confederation. Fighting continued into 1995, but the balance of power shifted toward the Muslim-Croat alliance. Massive NATO air strikes at Bosnian-Serb targets on August 30, 1995, brought the Serbs to a new round of peace talks. The siege of Sarajevo ended on September 15, 1995. Leaders of Bosnia, Croatia, and Serbia met in Dayton, Ohio, on November 21, 1995, to begin peace negotiations. The peace treaty they agreed upon in Dayton was signed in Paris on December 14, 1995.

The Yugoslav Wars of the early 1990s, which turned Zlata from a normal 11-year-old into a refugee, were a result of territorial conflicts that spurred the clash of arbitrary ethnic and religious borders. In order to understand the nationalistic hatreds behind such misery and destruction, we must look to the past. Discord over artificial borders plagued the Balkan

Peninsula for centuries and represented fundamental disputes over sovereignty, religion, and ethnicity. The area that the former Yugoslavia occupied has been at the center of these conflicts.

2

Fractured Empires and Troubled Borderlands

More than 1,000 years of history influenced the twentieth-century creation, and subsequent destruction, of Yugoslavia. The area's complex mosaic of peoples, languages, religions, and cultures that created arbitrary borders developed over centuries. For most of that period, the territories that later became Yugoslavia were subjected to warfare and forced migration, foreign intervention, and internal division. Beginning in the tenth century, Croats, Serbs, and finally Bosnians established viable, native states. Beginning in the fourteenth century, the powerful Ottoman and Habsburg empires controlled the area, ensuring that none of the native states would survive. To understand this disarray and the casting and recasting of arbitrary borders, we must look to a small population of South Slavs scattered across a difficult landscape.

Geography has played a vital role in the creation of economic, political, and cultural borders in the former Yugoslavia. Situated in the heart of the Balkan Peninsula, the former Yugoslavia has traditionally been a bridge or a battleground for empires and cultures. To the west, the narrow Adriatic Sea easily linked Yugoslavia to Italy and western Europe. To the north, the broad Danube River served as both an arbitrary border and a transportation corridor, opening Yugoslavia to central Europe. In the south, Greece connected Yugoslavia with Egypt via the island of Crete. Finally, to the east, the islands of the Aegean Sea provided easy access, in both directions, for colonists and invaders.

The area's complex terrain also served to enhance the creation of arbitrary borders. Mountainous terrain covers nearly 45 percent of the former Yugoslavia, with the Julian Alps reaching into Slovenia and the Balkan range stretching into Macedonia. More important, the rugged chain of the Dinaric Mountains traces a southeasterly course from Croatia to Herzegovina and Montenegro. The northeastern Dinaric range runs from Bosnia to western Serbia. For centuries, these craggy bands of mountains acted as barriers to political integration in the area, confining Mediterranean influence to the coast and leaving scattered land settlements isolated from each other. This range, as it turns south, also reinforced the separation between Eastern Orthodoxy and Western Catholicism that proceeded from Bosnia to the coast.

With the exception of the Danube, most of the Balkan rivers are not navigable year-round and thus were of little or no importance to the development of Yugoslavia. The Danube, however, is one of Europe's longest rivers, rising in southern Germany, cutting across the Balkan Peninsula, and emptying into the Black Sea. From prehistoric times, this great river acted as a natural highway, bringing invaders, settlers, and merchants into the area and linking Yugoslavia with central Europe to the west and Russia to the east. The Danube also served as the traditional route for peoples traveling westward from Asia. Thus, since recorded history, diverse and varied peoples have crisscrossed the lands of Yugoslavia, each leaving some trace of their culture and society behind.

Yugoslavia's arbitrary borders were not only geographic, but they were also created along ethnic lines. Indeed, the ethnography (ethnic makeup) of the former Yugoslavia is as complex as its terrain. Little is known about the ancient peoples that inhabited the lands of Yugoslavia. All we know comes from archaeological findings. We know that people in the Paleolithic period (2.5 million to 200,000 years ago) hunted and foraged in the mountains, valleys, and plains of the former Yugoslavia. In the Mesolithic period (8000 to 2700 B.C.), the use of tools expanded, and settlements emerged throughout the area.

The ancient Greeks established the first center of civilization on the Balkan Peninsula. In 600 B.C., they set up trading posts along the eastern Adriatic coast, and in the fourth century B.C., they established colonies there.

At the same time, Rome began making inroads onto the peninsula. In the third century B.C., Rome established a presence on the Adriatic and slowly began to dominate the Balkan Peninsula. The most important legacy of Roman domination was the empire's separation of its Eastern (Byzantine) and Western

(Roman) spheres in A.D. 395. This division separated Byzantium (renamed Greek Constantinople in A.D. 330) from Latin Rome and eventually split the Eastern Orthodox and Roman Catholic churches. When the Roman Empire divided in A.D. 395, the demarcation line between East and West cut across Yugoslavia. In the medieval period, this arbitrary border corresponded closely to the division between the Orthodox and Catholic worlds when the Byzantine Church split. This division separated the lands that were to become Yugoslavia and created a cultural divide that would separate East from West, Eastern Orthodox from Roman Catholic, and Serb from Croat and Slovene.

Because Catholicism arose in the West and Orthodoxy in the East, the difference between them is much greater than the differences between Catholicism and Protestantism or Judaism. Whereas Western religions tend to emphasize thought and action, Eastern religions emphasize beauty and magic. An Eastern Orthodox church service is rather mystical—almost a recreation of heaven on Earth. By comparison, Catholicism is austere and intellectual. Over centuries, such differences have engendered conflicting approaches to daily life that have strengthened the arbitrary borders between Balkan peoples of different faiths.

The most radical change in the ethnic composition of the area took place in the sixth and seventh centuries, as Slavic tribes poured onto the peninsula. The Slavs spoke an Indo-European language and organized themselves into sedentary clans that farmed and raised livestock. Gradually, these tribes settled into the central Balkans and developed as separate Slovenian, Croatian, Serbian, and Bosnian peoples.

As some of these Slavic tribes sought to unify into native states, arbitrary borders came to dominate the Yugoslav lands. Settling in the northwestern part of the Balkan region, the Slovenes did not form an independent political entity but rather became part of the Kingdom of the Franks in 748. As such, they were solidly Catholic. By the fourteenth century, the lands they inhabited came under Austrian (Habsburg) rule.

In contrast, those tribes that followed a southwestern track and converted to Christianity settled in Dalmatian coastal towns and distinguished themselves as Croats. In 910, Byzantine authorities recognized the ruler of the first Croatian state as Tomislav, who reigned until 928. Pope John X also confirmed Tomislav as king, thereby making Croatia independent of the Eastern Christian Church's center in Constantinople and ultimately placing it under the jurisdiction of the Roman Catholic Church. At its height in the eleventh century, the Great Croatian state included Dalmatia, Istria, Slovenia, Bosnia-Herzegovina, and Croatia proper.

Subsequent Croat kings cooperated closely with the growing Hungarian kingdom to the north as a hedge against foreign invasion. In 1089, the last in the line of kings descended from Tomislav died without an heir, and Croatia (together with the Adriatic coastal territory of Dalmatia) fell under the domination of Hungary. Threatened by Venice, both Croatia and Dalmatia welcomed Hungarian protection, and, in 1102, they also welcomed a Hungarian as the king of Croatia. Thus began the separate and unequal existence of Croatia within the Hungarian kingdom.

The exact nature of the agreement that placed a Hungarian king on the Croatian throne was to be disputed over the next several centuries. Nonetheless, from 1102, Croatia never again reestablished its once great kingdom. Motivated by fear of the East as manifested by the power of Constantinople (both Byzantine and, later, Turk), the Croats willingly accepted domination by Catholic popes, Hungarian kings, and finally Habsburg emperors.

The Serbs were another South Slavic group that inhabited the lands of the former Yugoslavia. Migrating onto the Balkan Peninsula in the seventh century, they settled in the central part, between the Drina and the Ibar rivers. The patriarchal Serb clans eventually migrated toward the Adriatic coast for winter pastures and the promise of trade. They converted to Christianity in the second half of the ninth century. A combination of

The founder of the Serbian state, Stefan Nemanja I, was a member of the Serbian Orthodox Church, which was established during his reign in the late twelfth century. In 1190, he founded the Church of the Virgin (pictured here) and the Church of the King, which together make up one of the largest and richest Serb monasteries, Studenica.

Byzantine and Bulgarian influences emanating from the south placed them in the realm of Eastern Orthodoxy rather than Latin Catholicism. Because the Serbs' nearest neighbors, the Croats, were Catholic, the borders that separated the two peoples went beyond geography.

The rise of a Serbian state is associated with the Nemanja Dynasty, which was founded near the end of the twelfth century by a tribal chieftain, Stefan Nemanja I (reigned 1168–1196). Stefan united Serb territory to the Adriatic, and his descendents ruled for the next two centuries. At the same time, a separate archbishopric was established in Serbia. In this way, Serbia became a kingdom with an autonomous Orthodox Church that used a Slavonic alphabet and a Slavic liturgy. Consequently, Serbian Orthodoxy became a main pillar of Serbian nationalism.

From the beginning, Serbia was among the most civilized king-doms in Europe. Whereas Stefan Nemanja could sign his name, the Holy Roman Emperor in Germany, Frederick I Barbarossa, could only manage a thumbprint.[6]

The medieval Serbian kingdom reached its height under Stefan Dusan (1331–1355). Dusan doubled the size of the Serbian territory, extending it from the Croatian border to the north, the Adriatic Sea to the west, the Aegean Sea to the south, and as far east as the gates of Constantinople. In 1346, he claimed for himself the title of tsar, or emperor, of Serbs and Greeks. Later, he added Albanians and Macedonians to the list.

Under Dusan, Serbia not only expanded its arbitrary geo-graphic borders, but it also established cultural borders, creating a uniquely Serbian culture. Church architecture flourished as it morphed from being crudely Byzantine into a blend of Western and Greek influences. Monasteries became centers of learning. Serbian literature began to reflect a feeling of national unity, and popular epics exclusively and peculiarly Serbian were sung in all parts of the kingdom.

Despite Dusan's ability to assemble an impressive empire, he failed to establish any centralized institutions that would sustain it. After his death in 1355, his weak successors were unable to maintain central control against domestic intrigues and foreign pressure. The Serbian lands became fragmented among compet-ing nobles as the feudal lords increased their power at the expense of the royal court. These nobles were willing to lose imperial territory for personal gain.

In 1371, however, fear of an invasion by the Ottoman Turks prompted the Serbian nobles to unify and to choose Knez (Prince) Lazar as the national leader. They enjoined upon him the task of meeting the Turkish threat. Even though during the previous 10 years the Ottoman Turks, under Murad I, advanced steadily northwest onto the Balkan Peninsula, heading toward Europe, Lazar received little support from the peoples of central and western Europe. Nonetheless, the Serbs resolved to stop the Turks and marched to meet them on the battlefield. On

(continued on page 23)

AMURATH, I.
*Third King of
The Turks.*
A.° 1350·

Murad I, depicted in this engraving, ruled the Ottoman Empire from 1359 to 1389 and brought most of the Balkans under his control. During his reign, he also established the janissary corps, which was made up of many non-Muslim South Slav boys taken prisoner by the Ottomans during their conquest of the Balkans.

THE BATTLE OF KOSOVO POLJE

On a hot June day in 1389, Serbian knights, arrayed in heavy chain mail, marched onto a huge plain known as Kosovo Polje, or Field of Blackbirds. Their armor, engraved in gold and silver, was dazzling in the bright sunlight, almost blinding to observers. Their helmets were adorned with magnificent plumes. They moved slowly, the weight of their fine armor exhausting them in the summer heat. By contrast, the lightly clad Turks moved swiftly on their tireless Mongolian ponies. Surprising the great Slavic army, they swept in on their fast mounts and picked the Serbs apart, butchering thousands and leaving the rotting corpses for vultures to devour.

Knez (Prince) Lazar had assembled a great contingent of Serbs, Croats, and Bosnians to halt the steady advance of the Turks across the Balkan Peninsula toward western Europe. Despite the immediate threat, all of the great western European nations were content to let the Slavic peoples face the Turks alone. Both Lazar and the Ottoman Empire's leader, Murad I, were killed on the day of the battle. From this defeat at the Kosovo Polje, Serbia was no longer able to function as a fully independent state and by the 1450s became incorporated into the Ottoman Empire.

Many Serbs feel that the battle at Kosovo Polje was the defining tragic moment in their history. For them, it has tremendous significance. They see it as a battle in which Serbs gave their lives to defend their Christian faith against the Muslim infidels. It also marks the beginning of 500 years of Ottoman rule under an Islamic empire that suppressed Christian religion and culture. Because no western European countries came to aid Serbia in fighting the Turks, the battle is also a symbol of the deep divide between the Catholic West and the Orthodox East. To this day, many Serbs feel the West betrayed them.

Nationalistic feelings relating to the Battle of Kosovo Polje have had important ramifications long after the 1300s. In the nineteenth century, many Serbs sought to reestablish the Serbian Empire and retake the area where the battle took place. Tensions between an expanding Serbia and Austria-Hungary were in large part responsible for starting World War I. In recent years, the breakup of Yugoslavia has caused a tremendous nationalist revival among Serbs. Once again, the Serbs' memory of their tragic defeat at Kosovo Polje has been a major part of this revival.

(*continued from page 20*)
September 26, 1371, a much smaller Turkish force launched a surprise attack on them at dawn, slaughtering great numbers. So great was the carnage that, to this day, the battlefield is called "the Serbs' destruction."

A much more devastating battle was yet to come—one that would destroy the remnants of the Serbian Empire and alter the political, cultural, and social borders of the entire Balkan Peninsula for the next 500 years. This great battle, fought on the Kosovo Plain near the Serbian-Bulgarian border, became known as the Battle of *Kosovo Polje* (Field of Blackbirds). Here, the Turks delivered the final defeat of the Serbs on June 28, 1389, leaving their bodies for vultures and ravens to devour. It was a culminating disaster for the South Slavs because it allowed the Turks ultimately to overtake the entire peninsula and establish their own arbitrary borders.

The story of this battle has been commemorated in songs, stories, legends, and epic poems to such an extent that we no longer know exactly what happened on the battlefield. Murad I was assassinated either during or after the battle. To avenge his death, the Turks began killing common soldiers as they were captured. After the battle, the Turks executed Prince Lazar and all the Christian princes. Serbs still sing songs and recite epic poems about those who fell at Kosovo Polje. The anniversary of the battle, June 28, remains a national holiday—*Vidovdan* (St. Vitus Day).

A final kingdom, Bosnia, arose between the Serbian and Croatian kingdoms and briefly outlasted them. Situated between the Eastern and Western churches, this area had a separate religious movement. Consequently, its religious borders were so ill defined that the population could not claim to be either Croat (Catholic) or Serb (Orthodox). To make matters more confusing for ethnic identification, after the Turks invaded and destroyed the Bosnian state in the fourteenth century, a large portion of this South Slav population converted to Islam. By the middle of the sixteenth century, nearly two-fifths of the entire population of Bosnia had converted to Islam.[7] Some of these converts had previously been Orthodox, others Catholic, and still others members of the Bosnian Church, which was independent of the latter two churches. The controversy over those conversions contributed greatly to the bloodshed in Sarajevo and elsewhere in Bosnia when Yugoslavia broke apart in the 1990s.

During the twelfth century, the Bosnian state achieved independence and rejected both Byzantine and Hungarian rule. Loosely constituted under a single governor, the Bosnian state consisted of a set of court officials, a state treasury, and an assembly of nobles who convened regularly. These nobles' social origins fit the pattern of local clan leaders similar to both the Serbs and the Croats. In fact, their ambiguous ethnic origins might have been more Croat than Serb, but this new ruling elite regarded itself as a separate Bosnian entity.[8] This arbitrary social border was also to have great significance in the twentieth-century wars.

The Bosnian state reached its height under Stefan Tvrtko (reigned 1353–1391). In 1377, Tvrtko was crowned king of the Serbs, Bosnians, and the Croats. This title reflects the large area that he controlled. He later added Herzegovina and Dalmatia to his possessions. After his death, a weak Bosnian state emerged, rent with internal division and vulnerable to foreign invasion. In the mid-fifteenth century, the powerful Hungarian Empire launched a determined campaign to force the Bosnian Church to come under the control of Roman papal authority and to establish its rule in the region. Bosnia capitulated. In 1463, however, an Ottoman Army easily conquered Bosnia and wrestled it out from under Hungarian control. Within 20 years, Herzegovina also fell to the Turks, and Bosnia-Herzegovina became a part of the Islamic Ottoman Empire.

By the end of the fourteenth century, the foundation for the modern Yugoslav state, consisting of Croatian, Serbian, and Bosnian kingdoms, had been set. Within this area, geographic borders and conquests overlapped. In the nineteenth and twentieth centuries, the national leaders looked back to this period and considered the maximum extension of their medieval kingdoms as the natural historical boundaries for their nations. As we have seen, though, these borders were arbitrary and fluctuated radically over time. At the same time, arbitrary cultural borders divided the area and left long-lasting cleavages that approximated the boundaries of the Eastern and Western Roman Empires. This is important because it split the area into two Christian churches: Eastern Orthodox and Roman Catholic. These arbitrary borders would be a source of political conflict in ensuing centuries.

3

Habsburg- and Ottoman- Imposed Borders

As we have seen, the histories of the South Slavic tribes that settled on the Balkan Peninsula have diverged since the earliest times. The Serbs followed Byzantium and adopted Orthodox religion and culture, whereas the Croats and Slovenes adhered to Roman Catholicism, and the Bosnians developed an autonomous Christian church that briefly came under the control of the Roman Catholic Church. In 1389, the Turks' victory at Kosovo Polje completed the separation and destroyed the Serbian Empire that had existed for nearly two centuries. Serbia and Bosnia-Herzegovina were ruled by the Ottoman Empire for more than 500 years, leaving Croatian and Slovenian lands under Habsburg rule. These two empires would assault the artificial barriers assembled by the earlier native kingdoms.

Turkish control of the Balkans from the Ottoman Empire's new capital at Constantinople began in 1389 and lasted until the Balkan Wars in 1913. The Ottoman state had been built on the concept of Holy War, with its primary objective the extension and defense of Islam. At its height, the Ottoman Empire was a centralized divine-right monarchy headed by a *sultan*, whose duty it was to extend Islam over as wide a territory as possible. A bureaucracy and military establishment with power that was not limited by local or provincial authorities served the sultan.

When the Turks conquered the Balkans, they imposed a centrally controlled regime of land tenure, tax collection, and native religious rights on all their possessions. The sultan's cavalry officers, the *Sipahis*, generally were given agricultural lands taken from newly conquered territories. Officers maintained themselves on this land by collecting a percentage of the food and livestock produced by the peasants living on it. These officers sent a portion of this "tax-in-kind" to Constantinople to help provision the state and army.

As long as the Ottoman Empire remained strong and continued to conquer new lands, the tax burdens on the peasantry were mild. Indeed, for a time, the Balkan peasants on Ottoman-controlled lands fared better than their western European counterparts. In addition to lighter taxes, peasants had hereditary use over a definite tract of land. The Sipahis had no legal right of lordship over the peasants. They had no right to evict the peasants or prevent them from moving and settling elsewhere. As long as the peasants paid their taxes, they could live in relative peace and autonomy.

Despite the emphasis on religious war, the Ottoman Turks were not interested in destroying local people or native religions. If a region did not resist, it could retain its religion and a large measure of autonomy. If it resisted, however, the Turks would

Expansion of Ottoman Empire, 1307–1481

Beginning in the 1300s, the Ottoman Empire began its conquest of the Balkans and quickly took control of most of present-day Bulgaria. The Ottomans next set their sights on the crumbling kingdom of Serbia. In 1389, Murad I defeated a Serbian force led by Prince Lazar at *Kosovo Polje* (Field of Blackbirds), ushering in an era of Ottoman influence that would last nearly 500 years.

enslave or massacre the population and confiscate all property as war booty. The Turks welcomed conversions to Islam, but did not force local populations to convert. However, non-Muslims paid more taxes. They also had to observe special restrictions, and they had an inferior social status. This is important because it set up new artificial social borders between those Slavic peoples who converted to Islam and those who did not.

A second artificial border resulting from Ottoman occupation separated people by their social position and function within the community. Members of the governing class, the *askeri* (literally, "military"), held the most privileged positions in society. They included high-ranking administrative authorities, military officials, and religious, educational, and legal professionals. The askeri also included high-ranking members of Christian society, such as patriarchs of the Orthodox Church. Below them were the *reaya*, or "protected flock." Most of the population, Christian and Muslim alike, fell into this category. Unlike the askeri, members of the reaya received few freedoms, had to pay taxes, and were restricted in their dress and lifestyle.

Slaves occupied the very bottom rung of the social hierarchy. The sultan used slaves largely to help in state administration and in key sections of the army. It was generally believed that slaves were the most loyal and trustworthy servitors, and the sultan relied on them with absolute assurance.

The sultan obtained some slaves as prisoners of war but purchased others. Usually, at least until the end of the seventeenth century, the sultan procured slaves through a system known as *devshirme*, meaning "to collect." Periodically, Ottoman officials went into the countryside to select slaves. Non-Muslim fathers (Muslims were exempt) who had sons between the ages of 8 and 20 had to present them for inspection. Boys were chosen on the basis of intelligence and looks.

Once the officials made their selections, they sent the boys in groups to Constantinople. There, they were examined, separated, and converted to Islam. The most promising stayed in Constantinople to be educated and trained as future administrators and trusted members of the sultan's household. The rest went to live with Turkish farmers, where they received language instruction and religious training. Most of these boys became *Janissaries*, the most effective fighting force anywhere in the world during this period.

Arbitrarily imposing the social category of "slave" on hundreds of thousands of boys had an ambiguous effect on the various South Slav people. The Muslims of Bosnia wanted to be included in this system of collection, because slave children gained the possibility of acquiring the best education and the

THE JANISSARIES

The Janissaries, a standing army of Christian soldiers, were the greatest military asset of the Ottoman Empire. Established in 1330, the Janissaries were non-Muslim prisoners of war and young Christian boys taken as slaves from conquered territory to provide military service for the sultan. Murad I (1319–1389) transformed this new military force into the elite personal army of the sultan. Janissaries, for all practical purposes, were the personal property of the sultan.

Initially, the sultan's administrators would randomly conscript a number of Christian boys and take them to be trained. Later, there were specific requirements for conscription. On average, one in five boys between the ages of 7 and 14 were taken from a locality, but in times of greater military need, greater numbers of boys were taken. Their training consisted of education in Islam and in the military arts. They trained under strict discipline and hard labor in nearly monastic conditions. Only those who proved strong enough earned the rank of a true Janissary at age 25.

The Janissaries were rewarded for their loyalty and ferocity in battle with grants of newly acquired land. Originally, they received pay only in wartime but could work as law enforcers or tradesmen during times of peace. Retired and invalid Janissaries even received pensions. Janissaries soon filled the most important administrative offices of the Ottoman Empire, enjoying high standards of living, exemption from paying taxes, and a respected social status. Janissaries' reputation increased to the point that by 1683, Sultan highest social standing in the empire. By contrast, some Christian Serbs and Croats tried to buy their children back, stressing the cruelty of taking children by force and converting them against their will. According to their Christian beliefs, conversion to Islam would lead to eternal damnation. Nonetheless, children taken in this way often rose to the top of the Ottoman state system. To be a slave of the sultan was an honor that brought with it high social standing and great material benefit.

Ottoman religious policy was one of the major factors that determined the historical development of the South Slavs and

Mehmet IV abolished conscription—and increasing numbers of Muslim Turkish families voluntarily enrolled their own sons into the corps.

By the early eighteenth century, the Janissaries had gained so much prestige and influence that they could dominate the government. Orchestrating palace coups, the Janissaries deposed or murdered more than a few sultans. Through mutinies and revolts, they were able to dictate policy and hinder Turkey's modernization. For example, in 1807, the Janissaries revolted and deposed Sultan Selium III, who was trying to modernize Turkey. As he tried to create a modern, European-style army, the Janissaries felt that their power was threatened and had him murdered.

Ultimately, the sultan realized he had to get rid of the Janissaries, in part because the Ottoman Empire could no longer afford to pay the salaries of 135,000 Janissaries who were not active military personnel. Moreover, the Janissaries presented a tremendous obstacle to modernizing Turkey's army. In 1826, it became clear that the sultan was forming a new army. On June 14 of that year, the Janissaries in Istanbul revolted, to stop the creation of this new army. This time, however, the cavalry and the population at large turned against them. Landowners and calvary units loyal to the sultan forced the Janissaries to retreat to their barracks. The sultan then ordered the artillery to fire into the barracks and surrounding buildings, causing massive casualties. Those Janissaries who survived were executed or banished, and within two years, the sultan confiscated all Janissary possessions, and the janissary corps ceased to be. This event is now called The Auspicious Incident.

enhanced religious borders in the Yugoslav lands. When Ottoman armies conquered a region, former civil administrators either fled or were killed. Since the church hierarchy usually remained, the Turks began using local religious leaders to perform governmental functions, as long as they submitted to Ottoman authority. Members of accepted faiths were organized into communities, called *millets*, and their clergy would oversee religious and internal legal affairs. Millets became the main institution for local religious and civil governance. Millets even administered justice as long as no Muslim was involved. By the eighteenth century, there was a Jewish millet, a Catholic millet, and a huge Orthodox millet. In this way, ethnic and religious borders were maintained as long at Ottoman authority was not challenged.

Ottoman control over the peoples of the future Yugoslavia also strengthened the artificial ethnic and economic borders that arose in the earlier period of native empires. One reason for this was that Ottoman rule was not uniform. Different parts of the empire were treated differently, depending on a province's distance from Constantinople and proximity to the frontier. Bosnia-Herzegovina was the Ottoman Empire's westernmost outpost. Therefore, the Turks fortified the province against its main enemy, the Habsburg Empire. To make the border more secure, the Turks granted concessions to the inhabitants of the area. Unlike nationalities subject in other regions of the empire, the Bosnian Serbs initially benefited from these concessions. The Croats living along the western and northern border also benefited from land grants received from the Turks.

A second reason the Ottoman period affected different areas differently was the amount of agricultural land within a region that could be given to the Sipahis. In some areas, such as Bosnia, Sipahis held significant amounts of land. In addition, unless they were away at war, these men usually lived on their land, forming an important element of Bosnian society. In addition, large numbers of Janissaries settled in Bosnia during the seventeenth and eighteenth centuries. Although some stayed in villages, the majority chose to live in Sarajevo, the largest Bosnian city at the time. Since the Janissaries did not receive regular pay, they had to find new occupations in Sarajevo. They became merchants and craftsmen and developed into the most influential political group in Sarajevo and other cities. The Janissaries' influence created new economic and social borders in Bosnian cities.

In Bosnia, large-scale conversions to Islam followed the Ottoman occupation. This is important because it blurred ethnic distinctions and resulted in tensions between Slavic groups as converts received social and economic benefits from the Ottoman Empire that Christians did not. It is also important because it eroded arbitrary borders between Christian converts to Islam and their Turkish overlords. The conversions created a situation in which local Slavs predominantly comprised the Muslim ruling elite that held all the political and economic power. During the eighteenth century, this group was able to use its power to infringe on peasant land, stealing unused or deserted areas. These Slavic Muslims also used their position as tax collectors to obtain property. The Orthodox Bosnian peasants, in turn, resented their rising obligations and intermittently rebelled against their Bosnian Muslim overlords.

To make the situation worse, Muslims only accounted for about 33 percent of the population, whereas the Orthodox population was about 43 percent and Catholics 20 percent of the total.[9] Consequently, the majority of Christian Slavic peasants were subordinate to the Muslim Slavic overlords. The Muslims favored Ottoman rule, whereas the Orthodox Christians felt drawn toward Serbia, which was overwhelmingly Orthodox, and the Catholics wanted to be a part of the Habsburg Empire or the Catholic Croat lands.

The geographic, social, and cultural borders of Bosnia would not change until the Habsburg Empire conquered and occupied this territory in the nineteenth century. Consequently, the seeds of future conflicts between rural Serbs or Croats and Muslims had been planted and the resulting tensions would erupt in bloodshed in the twentieth century. At the same time, no such antagonisms brewed in Sarajevo and other Bosnian cities. In the sixteenth century, Sarajevo's population was almost entirely Bosnian Muslims. In the ensuing centuries, the city welcomed Serb merchants, Croats, and Jews. Indeed, the mixed Christian and Muslim populations in urban Bosnia led to the overlapping and borrowing of religious traditions.

Unlike Bosnia, Serbia did not suffer a complex mixture of integration and oppression under Ottoman occupation. It took the Turks nearly 70 years of conquest, beginning with the battle of Kosovo Polje, to conquer the Serbian lands. During those years, Serbs migrated in droves to Bosnia, Herzegovina, and elsewhere, leaving the scattered lowlands in Kosovo empty. Albanians would ultimately move in and occupy this area. At the same time, the dense forests of the interior of Serbia discouraged the Ottomans from granting much land to the Sipahis, so that in rural Serbia, Muslim occupation had little impact. At the same time, in the cities, the Muslims established a significant presence. Consequently, local Serb leaders maintained control in the countryside but not in the cities. This is important because it strengthened the artificial border between Turk and Serb, Orthodox and Muslim, and rural and urban populations.

The Orthodox millet in Serbia was by far the largest and strongest in the entire Ottoman Empire and was a primary reason for the creation of a separate Serbian national identity. The millet system gave the Orthodox Church legal as well as religious powers. Under this system, the Serbian Orthodox Church gained independent authority. As a result, the Church had great power in keeping the idea of a separate Serbian national identity alive, thereby enhancing the artificial barrier between Serbs and other South Slav peoples.

Compared with Serbia and Bosnia, the Ottomans always had a very weak hold on Croatia. As we have seen, Croatia was an independent community from the tenth century until 1102, when the crown of Croatia was given to a Hungarian king. This crowning began a connection between Hungary and Croatia that lasted 800 years. Following an Ottoman victory over Hungary in the mid-1500s, most of Hungary and all of Croatia came under Ottoman control.

Turkish control in these lands was short lived, however. In 1699, the Treaty of Karlowitz restored Croatian lands to the (Austro-Hungarian) Habsburg Empire. Because the Habsburg government differed greatly from Turkish rule, Croatia developed along an entirely different path. Consequently, the historical experiences of the Croats diverged significantly from those of the Serbs or the Bosnians. This became important in the twentieth century, when all the South Slav lands were united into one Yugoslav state.

The Habsburg Empire was a collection of disparate lands loosely united through the Habsburg royal family, whose center was in Vienna, Austria. Habsburg territories were assembled through alliances and marriages, unlike the Ottoman pattern of invasion and occupation. Under Habsburg rule, the personal estates, historic rights, and autonomy of the local elites were usually preserved. Therefore, the local nobility, not the king or queen in Vienna, had direct control over the local population. Local nobles also had the power to levy taxes and recruit soldiers, which made imposition of a uniform system of governance throughout the empire impossible. This situation differed greatly from that of the Ottoman Empire, where sultans acquired territory through conquest. The Turks made no concessions to the local nobility, who were massacred unless they surrendered and converted to Islam. All people were subjects of the sultan, and all Ottoman lands were considered the sultan's personal property.

Likewise, the relationship between church and state and the process of establishing religious borders was much more complicated in the Habsburg Empire than in the Ottoman possessions. In the Ottoman Empire, the Sultan headed the church as well as the government. Similarly, the Orthodox Church combined religious and political duties that the millet system maintained under the Turks.

Further, in lands under Ottoman control, the Christian and Muslim churches tolerated each other and did not wage outright religious war against each other. Because both religions cooperated within the Ottoman Empire, Orthodox hatreds were aimed

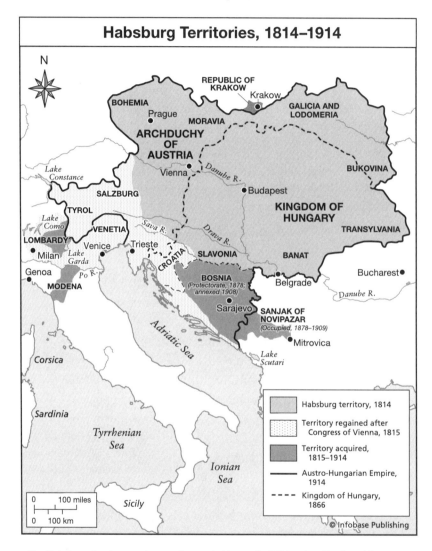

The Habsburg Empire rose to prominence in Europe in 1526, when Ferdinand I was elected king of Bohemia and Hungary. From that point forward, the empire grew through the combination of royal alliances and marriages until it eventually encompassed more than half of Europe.

outward at Catholic encroachment rather than inward toward Muslims. Over time, the arbitrary border separating the two Christian churches—Orthodox and Catholic—became much stronger and more dangerous in all the Yugoslav lands than that between Christianity and Islam. This separation between Christian churches became the cause of many problems and conflicts as foreign powers sought to unify Yugoslavia in the twentieth century.

The history of imperial occupation of Croatia following the 1699 Treaty of Karlowitz is even more complex than that of Bosnia or Serbia. Until the end of the eighteenth century, what is now modern-day Croatia was divided into five parts—three sections were part of the Habsburg Empire and two belonged to Venice. These arbitrary borders, and the different historical experiences they represent, acted as barriers to the creation of a unified Croatian state and further complicated an already complex religious and ethnic landscape.

To protect itself from Ottoman advance, the Habsburg Empire established a military frontier in Croatia that the Habsburg monarch ruled directly. This artificial border created a line of defense that incorporated half of Croatia and all of Slovenia. In battles between Austria and the Turks, the war-devastated military frontier became depopulated as locals fled to safer areas. This depopulation led to a search for new settlers, who received special land grants in return for military service. The bulk of these new settlers were Serbian Orthodox refugees who moved northward in advance of the Ottoman armies. They created Orthodox Serb settlements along the entire Croatian frontier, further complicating arbitrary borders between Serbs and Croats.

A small group of nobles that was Croatian in nationality and Catholic in religion dominated Croatian political life. The Habsburg Empire allowed the Croats to administer their internal affairs through the Sabor (or Parliament) in the Croatian capital of Zagreb. A Croatian governor appointed by the emperor oversaw the Sabor. Because of its proximity to Hungary and the melding of the Habsburg Empire with Hungary, the large landowners were both Hungarian and Croat. The Croatian nobility constantly struggled against both Vienna and Hungary for control over Croatian counties. They sought to maintain their feudal privileges over their lands and their enserfed peasants. The Catholic Church also had tremendous political power in Croatia, a condition that would greatly strain relations with the Orthodox Serbs in the future.

Arbitrary social borders accompanied these political borders. As with the rest of the Yugoslav lands, the majority of the population were peasants. In general, peasants paid taxes and provided labor services to the landlord, the state, and the church. The landlord controlled the land, of course, but also the police, the judicial system, and tax collection. One can imagine the abuses that resulted from this type of system. A wide social border separated peasant from noble. The upper classes felt no affinity for the peasants, even though both were Croatian. An old Croat saying claims that a noble would sooner admit his horse into his house than a peasant. Indeed, so great was the nobles' disdain for the peasants that, until the nineteenth century, the educated classes rejected the Slavic language used by the peasants; they instead used Latin for administration and German for polite conversation.

Despite common origins as South Slavic tribes, by the beginning of the nineteenth century, the peoples of the Yugoslav lands were divided by arbitrary social, cultural, and political borders. Historically, imperial control varied greatly by region and further divided them. Perhaps the most powerful and most divisive influence was religion, as local populations adopted Catholicism, Orthodoxy, or Islam. Finally, as the two great empires, Ottoman and Habsburg, began to decline in the nineteenth century, the Yugoslav peoples were further divided by a new arbitrary border—nationalism.

4

Rising Nationalism and the Eastern Question

For the Yugoslav peoples, the nineteenth century was an era of collapsing empires and rising nationalism. The changes that would radically alter the arbitrary borders in the Yugoslav lands had their roots in the slow disintegration of the Ottoman Empire and the increasing intervention in the Balkans by the European powers. Together, these two issues created the central feature of Yugoslav diplomacy throughout the nineteenth century—the Eastern Question.

The Eastern Question revolved around one problem: What should happen to the Balkans when the Ottoman Empire disappeared as the fundamental political entity in southeastern Europe? The European powers (France, Britain, Russia, and Austria) approached each crisis in the Balkans with the hope that their own countries would emerge with maximum advantage. This led one or another power to support revolutionary change sometimes, and at other times to support the status quo. At no time, however, did they consider the wishes of the South Slavic people.

By the nineteenth century, the Ottoman Empire still possessed most of the Balkans, as well as vast areas in Asia and Africa. Although it still had the appearance of a great empire, it was actually crumbling and quite fragile. A succession of military defeats characterized the preceding century, which resulted in a loss of territory for the Ottoman Empire. This military weakness and loss of lands created internal disorder, as masses of South Slav peasants expressed their discontent with rising taxes and ineffective government. Authorities in the Balkans failed to keep order, so conditions of local anarchy arose throughout the area. Adding to the chaos, gangs of bandits and disgruntled unpaid soldiers roamed the countryside, robbing the local population and plundering whole villages. The breakdown of the Ottoman central government was paralleled by the rise in power of local authorities who gained effective control of their regions and removed themselves from the sultan's administration.

The clear and obvious need was for military reform. The main military problem was the Janissary units. Its members,

Sultan Selim III ruled the Ottoman Empire from 1789 to 1807 but was unable to revitalize the once-great power largely due to resistance by the Janissaries. Shortly after Selim was deposed, the Serbs were able to break away from Ottoman rule and establish an autonomous Serbia.

dispersed throughout the empire, became a source of political disorder and intrigue. As early as the eighteenth century, the Janissaries, largely discontent over receiving little or no wages, were no longer very loyal to the sultan. Until the sultan disbanded them in 1826, they were the main source of political instability in the Balkans. Because they were the most effectively organized and armed group in Constantinople and in provincial cities, the Janissaries often orchestrated court intrigues and political coups. Indeed, throughout the eighteenth century, they repeatedly demonstrated their skill in controlling or overthrowing the sultan or various provincial governors.

By the nineteenth century, the situation had worsened to the point that the Ottoman Empire was basically a government in name only. The impotence of the government became clear

THE TREATY OF KARLOWITZ AND THE TREATY OF BERLIN

Two treaties had important ramifications for the establishment of arbitrary borders in the lands of Yugoslavia: the Treaty of Karlowitz (1699) and the Treaty of Berlin (1878). The Treaty of Karlowitz concluded the Austro-Ottoman War of 1683–1697, in which the Ottoman Empire was defeated. Following a two-month congress between the Ottoman Empire and the European powers, the treaty was signed on January 26, 1699.

In the Treaty of Karlowitz, the Ottoman Empire permanently surrendered important territories to Christian powers. It ceded Slavonia and Croatia, along with other lands, to Austria, whereas most of the Croatian coast passed to Venice. This treaty marks the beginning of Ottoman decline on the Balkan Peninsula and made the Habsburg Empire the dominant power in the region. The weakening of the Ottoman Empire ultimately triggered national revolutions that erupted in the nineteenth century, fostered great power rivalry for influence and territory in the Balkans, and strengthened the arbitrary borders separating those Slavic peoples who came under Ottoman rule from those under Habsburg rule.

A second treaty that was to have wide-ranging implications was the Treaty of Berlin in 1878. The Treaty of Berlin is an important landmark in the formation of the Balkan national states. It is the single most important document for the national liberation movements in the Balkans. The treaty recognized the complete independence of Serbia, Romania, and Montenegro. An autonomous Bulgaria was established, but with a much reduced territory. The when Sultan Selim III tried to reform and revitalize the empire between 1789 and 1807. He sought to reorganize the bureaucracy and imperial administration, to revamp education, and to establish a modern Western-style army. The Janissaries strongly resisted these reforms, fearing that such changes might undermine their power. Unfortunately, a Janissary strangled Sultan Selim III to death, thereby ending his attempts at reform.

The failure to reform the Ottoman Empire was extremely important for the South Slav peoples, because it stimulated two trends that would again alter the arbitrary borders of the

Ottoman province of Bosnia-Herzegovina was placed under Austro-Hungarian occupation, while still formally remaining part of the Ottoman Empire.

The Treaty of Berlin was a turning point in that it left all the Balkan peoples (except Albania) with independent or autonomous states. An essential feature of the treaty, however, was its disregard of national and ethnic considerations. Consequently, every one of the Balkan people was left thoroughly dissatisfied: Bulgarians were embittered by the partition of their country; Serbs were angered by the administrative advance of Austria into Bosnia-Herzegovina; Romanians because they lost territory to Russia; and Greeks because they did not get any territory. The Treaty of Berlin exemplifies the weakness of arbitrarily created borders—arbitrary divisions often lead to arbitrary violence.

Ultimately, the Treaty of Berlin caused dissention and strife among the Balkan peoples. Now that Bosnia-Herzegovina was in the hands of the Austrians, in order to create a Greater Serbia, the Serbs were forced to turn southward into Macedonia. The result was a suicidal three-cornered conflict that poisoned inter-Balkan relations and fomented anarchy and bloodshed in Macedonia until World War I and even later. For the Balkan people, the Treaty of Berlin meant frustration of national aspirations and future wars. The direct and logical outcome was the Serbian-Bulgarian War of 1885, the annexation of Bosnia in 1908, the two Balkan wars of 1912–1913, and the murder of Archduke Franz Ferdinand in 1914, which ignited World War I.

Yugoslav lands: the intrusion of the great European powers into the affairs of the Balkan peoples and the awakening of national consciousness among the subject nationalities.

In the nineteenth century, the Ottoman Empire and the European powers had a very different relationship than they had in earlier times, when Turkish armies twice besieged Vienna. The turning point was the Treaty of Karlowitz in 1699, when the European powers forced the defeated Turks to give up some of their conquered lands. It was the first time the Turks had lost a battle and had to make concessions to a European power. After 1699, the Turks never again threatened Europe. On the contrary, the European powers were now faced with the opposite problem: how to fill the power vacuum created in the Balkans and the Near East by the declining Ottoman Empire. This question—the Eastern Question—dominated nineteenth-century international relations.

Austria and Russia first took advantage of the weakening Ottoman Empire by conquering territories along the Danube River and the Black Sea. During the late eighteenth and early nineteenth centuries, Britain remained relatively uninvolved in the Balkans and relatively unconcerned by Russia's advance onto the Balkan Peninsula. This was in part because Britain's prolonged war with France prohibited Britain from paying much attention to Russia's incursions onto the peninsula. At the same time, Britain carried on a very profitable trade with Russia and did not see Russia as a threat. During the course of the nineteenth century, however, the commercial and political situation changed. Britain's trade with Russia declined at the same time that Britain began lively trade relations with the Turks.

The British Foreign Office increasingly began to view Russia's designs on gaining Yugoslav territory as counter to British imperial interests. Therefore, throughout the second half of the nineteenth century, Britain strove to prop up the ailing Ottoman Empire against Russian aggression. Consequently, Russian diplomacy generally was anti-Turkish, whereas British diplomacy was rather pro-Turkish.

France also played a vital role in the Balkans. Over the course of the nineteenth century, France generally sided with Britain to prop up the failing Ottoman Empire. The French did so not out of any kind of mutual interest but out of a mutual desire to block Russian expansion in the Balkans. Indeed, during the Crimean War (1853–1856), France and Britain fought together to defend the Turks against Russia and continued to cooperate on most crucial issues until World War I.

The other great power interested in the Balkans was Austria. Austria alternated between two contradictory policies after the stunning gains made by the Treaty of Karlowitz. Sometimes Austria attacked the Ottoman Empire as a weak neighbor ripe for partition. At other times, Austria supported the Ottomans as a useful bulwark against the menacing advance of Russia. Generally, however, Austria sided with Britain in supporting the status quo in the Balkans. Both Austria and Britain feared that any change might strengthen Russia. Austria saw Russia as particularly dangerous because it feared that the many Slavic peoples living in the Habsburg Empire might be attracted to Russian national and religious propaganda. Such propaganda increased the possibility of a general Slavic revolt against Habsburg rule.

These four European powers—Britain, Russia, Austria, and France—to a considerable degree determined the casting and recasting of arbitrary borders throughout the Balkan Peninsula in the nineteenth century. Their conflicting interests help to explain why the failing Ottoman Empire managed to survive until World War I. The involvement of these countries in the area, aided by the weakness of the Turks, prompted the awakening of national consciousness of the South Slav peoples and gave birth to the idea of a unified Yugoslav state.

Equally as important as the involvement of the great powers in transforming the arbitrary geographic and political borders were developments that transformed static theocratic South Slav societies into nationalistic communities longing for revolutionary changes in government and law. For nearly all of the 500 years that the Ottoman Empire ruled the South Slav peoples, the millet system preserved traditional religious and cultural practices among native communities. As a result, the Orthodox Church had a great amount of power at the local level. And for nearly all of those 500 years, the Orthodox hierarchy had branded everything Western as "Latin" and hence heretical and repugnant. Yet in the nineteenth century, national awakenings gradually undermined Orthodox hegemony, and theocracy gave way to the age of nationalism.

One reason for the change was trade. The rapid growth in the volume of trade in the eighteenth century started the transition from theocracy to nationalism. Toward the end of the eighteenth century, Western demand for corn and cotton rose dramatically. These crops, grown on the plains of the Balkan Peninsula, were exported to western Europe. The expansion of trade led to a new social class: merchants, artisans, and mariners who had very different attitudes toward the West than did the Orthodox officials who had dominated previously. This emerging merchant class provided new social and political borders and introduced new ideas into the political landscape of the Balkans. Some tradespeople visited western European cities in the course of commercial operations. They observed the rule of law, political institutions, economic prosperity, and intellectual life not apparent in the Balkans.

Many in the Balkan merchant class saw Europe as a model to be imitated and eagerly sought to bring home "European Enlightenment." They shipped home books and equipment, sent young fellow countrymen to foreign universities, and financed the publication of European books and newspapers.

These economic and intellectual developments had political repercussions: Merchants who supported and spread ideas of the Enlightenment tended to support movements for political liberation. In essence, they sought to break down the arbitrary borders that subjected them to foreign rule and religious oppression. It is no accident that Serb pig dealers were the leaders in the Serbian revolt against the Ottoman Empire.

Peasants supported the new revolutionary leaders because of a change in land tenure that roused them to action. As we have seen, when the Turks conquered a region, they divided the best lands among themselves and gave it to the Sipahis. The sultan could take these lands back if landholders did not perform specified military duties. Peasants were allowed to work the land and could pass it on to their children, as long as they paid taxes. In the nineteenth century, however, landholders took advantage of the weakness of the Ottoman government by increasing taxes and evicting peasants who refused to pay. Rising peasant debt forced the formerly free peasants into serfdom. In this way, the landlords exploited the peasantry for the production of export commodities, mostly cotton and corn. Fed up, the peasants backed the nationalist revolutionaries. The resulting wars of liberation changed the artificial borders of the Yugoslav lands.

The Serbs were the first of the South Slav peoples to take up arms against the Turks. The revolt began in 1804 because of the breakdown in Ottoman administration. Ordinarily, peasants enjoyed self-government in their villages—they had virtually no contact with the sultan's officials. Their tax burden was light and they could freely move to another estate at any time. It was in the Sipahis' best interests to treat the peasants well, so they would stay and work the land. In the early 1800s, however, the system started to break down. As mentioned earlier, landlords began to exploit the peasants, increasing their tax burdens and forcing them into serfdom.

At the same time, the Janissaries began to openly defy the sultan. They even began seizing the Sipahis' land and exploiting Serb peasant tenants even more ruthlessly than the landlords did. To control the situation, the sultan's representative in Serbia, the Pasha Hadji Mustafa, armed the Serbs so they could protect themselves against the Janissaries. His gamble failed, and in the end, the Janissaries murdered him.

What followed was a bloody reign of terror as the Janissaries exacted retribution upon the Serbs. The Serbs appealed to

Constantinople, but the sultan could do nothing, so the Serbs took up arms in desperation.

Karageorge, or Black George, led the Serbs in revolt. He was a wealthy hog dealer who also was a first-rate military commander. Within months, he managed to defeat three Turkish armies, and by 1806, he took Belgrade, the capital of Serbia, from the Turks. Already engaged in a war with Russia and Britain at the time, the sultan, in order to quickly end the revolt, agreed to Karageorge's demands to create an autonomous Serbia under Ottoman rule. At the same time, the Russians offered the Serbs money and support if they continued fighting. Karageorge had to choose between Serbian autonomy under the Turks or cooperation with the Russian tsar with the goal of complete independence for Serbia. He chose the latter and on July 10, 1807, he agreed to sign a Serbian-Russian alliance.

Karageorge soon regretted his decision. Three days earlier, on July 7, the Russian tsar signed a treaty with Napoleon, making Russia and France allies. Since the Turks already had allied with France, Russia was now allied with the Turks, which ended their support of Serbia. This left the Serbs all alone to face the Ottoman Empire. Within a few years, the Turks exacted bloody revenge on the Serb revolutionaries. They conducted wholesale massacres, seized lands from Serb peasants, and gave the Janissaries free reign to do as they wished with the Serbs.

So great was the terror and spoilage that another revolt broke out in 1814. This one ultimately succeeded and forced an Ottoman concession of limited autonomy for the Serbs. The Turks recognized the Serbian leader of this second revolt, Miloš Obrenović (who gained power after Karageorge fled following the Serb defeat in Belgrade), as knez (prince). Ottoman administration and garrisons remained as before, but the Serbs could hold a national assembly and retain their arms. Obrenović ruled the new Serbian state until 1839, when his son took over and ruled until 1842. The latter was ousted by Alexander Karageorgevic, the son of Karageorge, the leader of the first revolt. During the next several decades, these two dynasties—

Mihailo Obrenović III, pictured here in 1850, succeeded his father, Miloš Obrenović, as ruler of Serbia in 1839. In 1842, he was deposed by Alexander Karageorgević but returned to the throne after Karageorgević's death in 1860, only to be assassinated in 1868.

Obrenović and Karageorgević—succeeded one another as rulers of Serbia and later Yugoslavia, until the Communist takeover in World War II.

These uprisings are important for two reasons. The ruthless reprisals that followed the first uprising linked it in Serbian historical memory to the medieval empire's defeat in 1389 at the Battle of Kosovo Polje. The Serbs revived the bloody legend of heroic defiance and cruel defeat in songs and epic poetry. Second, the revolts led to the idea that restoring a Serbian state would be the only way to end Serb suffering at the hands of the Turks. Serbia's national aims included recovering Kosovo and other ancient lands (such as Bosnia, Herzegovina, and Montenegro), as well as the unification of all Serbs into a single South Slavic state. As the Ottoman Empire declined, rebellion also broke out in Bosnia-Herzegovina.

As we have seen, the social borders in Bosnia were not related in any simple way to the division between Muslims and Christians: According to an 1879 census, Bosnia contained just a little more than 500,000 Orthodox believers, 448,000 Muslims, and 200,000 Catholics.[10] True, a Muslim elite controlled most of the wealth and power in Bosnia, but most Muslims were actually peasants, not large landholders. During hard times, these Bosnian Muslim peasants shared all the miseries and hardships of Bosnian Christian peasants. Moreover, the Bosnian Muslims were also Slavs, like their Christian neighbors. Consequently, the most important conflicts in Bosnia during the nineteenth century occurred between the Bosnian Muslim elite and their Ottoman overlords.

In contrast to the situation in Serbia, the Ottoman hold on Croatia was always weak. Croatian lands fell under the control of Hungary and, later, the Austro-Hungarian Empire. In the nineteenth century, the Habsburg Empire started to decline, and the Hungarians began agitating for greater independence from Austria. This triggered Croatian nationalism and gave rise to a movement for an independent Croatian state.

One of the most important leaders to emerge in Croatia in the second half of the nineteenth century was the Catholic bishop Joseph Strossmayer, who attempted to unite the South Slavs. Though German by birth, he was a great champion of Croat national rights. He sought to establish an autonomous Yugoslav state, with Croatia at the center, within the Habsburg framework. Even though arbitrary religious and cultural borders separated the Croats, Serbs, and Bosnians, Strossmayer considered them to be all one nationality—Yugoslav. In an attempt to dismantle some of the arbitrary borders dividing the Yugoslavs, Strossmayer subsidized scholars, built schools, and established a seminary, a national university, and an art gallery.

At the same time, an extremist nationalist group emerged to counter Strossmayer's idea of a genuine Yugoslav state. It adopted an all-Croatian program, rather than a united Yugoslavia, and it aimed for Croatian domination rather than equality among all South Slavs. This Catholic-oriented party viewed Serbs as turncoat Croats who subscribed to heresy (Orthodoxy). The Hungarian governor of Croatia fueled antagonisms between Serbs and Croats by granting special privileges to the Serbian Orthodox Church and to the Serb minority living in Croatia. His ploy worked, and violent clashes between Serbs and Croats erupted and continued throughout the 1890s.

By the turn of the century, the fate of the Yugoslav peoples remained uncertain. Both the Habsburg and Ottoman Empires were in serious decline, which had a dramatic effect on the South Slav populations. What precisely would emerge from the ruins of these two great empires would be determined by both the fluidity and inflexibility of arbitrary Balkan borders. It would take two Balkan wars and a worldwide conflict to unify, however briefly, the South Slavs into the first Yugoslavian state.

5

New Arbitrary Borders and Yugoslav Unity

As the twentieth century dawned, change was in the air in the Balkans. Indeed, the year 1903 seemed to usher in a new era. That year, the new Karageorgević Dynasty came to power in Serbia and promised to make the independent state a genuine parliamentary democracy. Increasingly, South Slavs looked to this new constitutional monarchy in Serbia as an alternative to imperial domination. That same year, an uprising challenged Ottoman rule in Macedonia, and the year also marked the end of the 20-year regimes of Habsburg administrators in both Croatia and Bosnia-Herzegovina. All across the South Slav lands of the Habsburg Empire, ethnically based political parties questioned the existing political order and debated the future of Yugoslav unification. Even the word *Yugoslavia* passed into common usage.[11]

A new form of imperialism accompanied by economic changes at the end of the nineteenth century played an important role in the shifting political borders. Imperialism is often defined as the political or economic control, either direct or indirect, of one state or people over another. In this sense, imperialism is as old as history itself. Certainly imperialism has been a constant factor in the affairs of the South Slavs. In the last quarter of the nineteenth century, however, as European countries became industrialized, a new type of imperialism emerged that was intimately linked to western European economic expansion. Unlike earlier forms of imperialism in the Balkans, this new imperialism took the form of forceful and pervasive economic penetration that also involved government protection of private investment. Consequently, European governments encouraged loans to "friendly" states and discouraged loans to "hostile" ones. This stimulated significant tensions between European powers competing for control in the Balkans.

Seeking new markets for industrial goods and new territories for capital investment, the Western powers increasingly vied for economic advantages in the Balkans. By the late nineteenth century, German, French, British, Austrian, and Italian financiers had descended on the Balkans, eager to gain large returns on their money. They invested huge amounts of capital in the form of government loans on projects that ultimately transformed the Balkan infrastructure: rail systems, roads, ports, docks, irrigation works, and power plants.[12] In addition to transforming the Balkan infrastructure, such projects led directly to an influx of Western goods and placed Balkan governments under a tremendous burden of debt to European investors.

The new imperialism had a tremendous impact on the daily lives of South Slav peasants. Rural peasants still made up the majority of the population of the future Yugoslav lands. In Serbia, for example, in 1914, 84 percent of the population was engaged in agriculture, 7 percent in industry, 5 percent in government, and 4 percent in trade.[13] At the same time, the improvement of transportation facilities generated by foreign investments helped the growth of industry. Milling was the most important industry, followed by meatpacking, brewing, woolen textiles, and mining. In short, Balkan industry centered almost entirely on the processing of raw materials and on agricultural products produced locally.

Although some peasants benefited from the economic upswing created by the new imperialism, the majority did not. One reason was that industrial growth remained limited—in 1910, less than 10 percent of the population engaged in industry. Another reason was the sharp increase in population—more than one percent population growth per year with no means to buy more land or use more efficient agricultural methods to increase crop yields. The net result was mounting population pressure on the land that led to the fragmentation of peasant property. Added to population growth, the custom of dividing a family's property equally among all the sons further fragmented small landholdings. As individual landholdings shrank, the majority of rural inhabitants fell into poverty.

The rapid rise in government expenditures and debts intensified rural poverty in the late nineteenth century. Owing to the mounting costs of a state bureaucracy and the armed forces, government expenditures rose dramatically. Increasing expenditures

During the late nineteenth century, many South Slav peasants were adversely affected by the heavy taxes placed on consumer goods by the Yugoslavian government. Due to their inability to afford basic commodities, such as tobacco and salt, peasants sometimes turned to begging.

meant increasing debts, as governments borrowed from European powers. Increasing foreign control over national finances accompanied increasing indebtedness. The end result was higher taxes on commodities such as tobacco, salt, and alcohol. The more prices of commodities rose, the less peasants could afford to buy.

These economic changes had quite an impact on the South Slav peasants. They had freed themselves from their Turkish overlords and feudal obligations in the first half of the nineteenth century only to find themselves at the mercy of village moneylenders and merchants and obligated through high taxes to support an expensive state apparatus. Peasants needed money to pay taxes and to buy the Western manufactured goods now available. Consequently, they had to produce more and sell the surplus on the domestic and international market.

New social and political borders resulted from these economic changes. By the end of the nineteenth century, growing stratification between the classes divided rural peasants along economic lines. With the growth of a money economy and a credit establishment, successful peasants were able to borrow money from government institutions at a low interest rate. Most peasants could not qualify for low-interest government loans, because they could not provide the security necessary to procure such a loan. Those who could get government loans borrowed at 6 percent interest and lent money to less fortunate peasants at 12, 36, or even 120 percent.[14] Thus, wealthy peasant moneylenders could afford to send their sons to school, or even the university, which enhanced career opportunities and prestige for the family. Poor peasant families could not even dream of such opportunities for their sons. This class stratification caused considerable tension within the villages. The moneylenders tended to be ruthless and were generally despised by the poor peasants. In referring to the moneylenders, a common peasant saying was, "Our lice eat us."[15]

An increasing gulf between the city and the countryside intensified another social border. Under Turkish domination, Turkish officials, the army, and various foreign artisans and merchants occupied the cities, whereas local ethnicities generally occupied the rural areas. This division persisted even after independence. One reason was that the peasants viewed the new bureaucratic class in the cities as expensive, inefficient, corrupt, and generally useless. Indeed, peasants thought that independence, in addition to freedom from Turkish domination, should mean no more interference from, or obligations to, the city.

Cultural differences reinforced this arbitrary border between city and country. Urban residents were by far more literate than rural inhabitants. In the countryside, less than 75 percent of the children attended school, and villagers were overwhelmingly illiterate. In contrast, state officials and bureaucrats who had contact with peasants were usually well educated. These urban dwellers considered themselves superior to their rural neighbors and looked with contempt upon the illiterate peasants.

The pre-World War I economic advance, although serving to create or intensify social divisions within the South Slav lands, had a political component that helped in the process of creating a modern Yugoslav nationalism. Indeed, the most important development among the South Slavs at the turn of the century was the increasing cooperation between Serbs and Croats within the Habsburg lands. One reason for this was because Croatia received a new Hungarian governor. Lacking diplomatic skills, the new governor often resorted to using brute force, which drove Serbs and Croats to cooperate in self-defense. At the same time, the new ruling dynasty in Serbia, the Karageorgevic᷄ Dynasty, was openly anti-Austrian and pro-Yugoslavian. This enticed the Habsburg Slavs to reject Austria-Hungary and to look toward Serbia as their hope for the future.

Ironically, internal divisions within the Habsburg Empire also fostered greater Yugoslav unity. From 1903 to 1907, conflicts between Hungary and Austria allowed for a brief loosening of political control in Croatia. During this thaw, numerous political parties sprang into existence. Two of them played a major role in the creation of a future Yugoslavia. The Croatian People's Peasant Party (CPPP), founded in 1904 by Stjepan and Ante Radic᷄, was based on Pan-Slavic (all-Slavic) nationalism. It claimed that all Slavs were brothers and that evil Catholic and Orthodox priests had created false antagonisms between Serbs and Croats. The CPPP put forth a program of cooperation between Serbs and Croats in Croatia.

The other political party that became important in unifying the South Slavs was the Serbian Independents, representing Serbs in Croatia. The leaders of this party encouraged cooperation with Croats and forged a Serb-Croat Coalition in 1905. Advocating Serb autonomy within Croatia rather than genuine Yugoslav unification, the Coalition nonetheless presented a "new course" of ethnic cooperation and proposed a union of Serbs and Croats into one nation.

Even though Austria-Hungary had occupied Bosnia-Herzegovina in 1878, the outright annexation of the provinces in 1908 greatly accelerated Serb-Croat cooperation. When the Habsburgs had first occupied Bosnia-Herzegovina, the Ottoman Empire was in decline. At that time, the population consisted of 43 percent Orthodox Serbs, 39 percent Bosnian Muslims, and 18 percent Catholic Croats.[16] Under Ottoman control, the Bosnian Muslims were the most privileged group, with 6,000 to 7,000 Muslims owning most of the land and wielding great political power.

When the Habsburgs occupied Bosnia-Herzegovina, they did not introduce any fundamental social changes. They did not challenge the Muslim ruling class and allowed the existing feudal class to continue. This meant that thousands of serfs tilled individual plots using archaic methods, which resulted in extreme rural poverty and agrarian unrest. Consequently, tension existed along arbitrary divisions between Muslim overlords and their Christian tenants. The situation also gave rise to political conflict between the imperial authority and growing Serb-Croat nationalism.

When the Habsburgs annexed (took over) Bosnia-Herzegovina in October 1908, it raised the ire of South Slav nationalists, who vowed to recover the two provinces at any cost. The loudest protest came from Serbia. Serbs everywhere were outraged by the annexation. They felt that Bosnia was Serbian land wrongfully seized first by Turkish power and now by the Habsburgs, and ruled over by renegade Slavs. In Belgrade, the Serbian capital, the press called for war. Even in Zagreb, the capital of Croatia, citizens showed their support by rioting.

Following the annexation of Bosnia-Herzegovina, the growing student populations in both Zagreb and Sarajevo turned from frustration to terrorism. The newly formed Croatian-Serbian Radical Youth Movement staged student strikes at Zagreb University and tried unsuccessfully to assassinate high-ranking Austrian officials. In addition to a commitment to terrorism, this student group clung to a romantic, revolutionary

the province. By the time the European powers met in December 1912 to decide on the borders of the larger Serbia, the Serbs had already slaughtered nearly 20,000 Kosovar Albanians. The Serbs

Second Balkan War, 1913

0   100 miles
0   100 km

Budapest

Danube R.

AUSTRO-HUNGARIAN EMPIRE

Prut R.

RUSSIA

BOSNIA-HERZEGOVINA   Belgrade   Bucharest   **ROMANIA**

Sarajevo   **SERBIA**   *Danube R.*

BULGARIA   *Black Sea*

MONTENEGRO   Philippopolis (Plovdiv)

Cetinje   Scutari (Shkodër)   Skopje   Constantinople

Adriatic Sea   Adrianople (Edirne)

Monastir (Bitola)   Enos   O T T O M A N

ALBANIA   Salonika   E M P I R E

Corfu   *Aegean Sea*

G R E E C E

N   Athens

Countries aligned against Bulgaria

Land gained under Treaty of Bucharest

Maritime boundaries   Crete   *Dodecanese Is.*

Mediterranean Sea

© Infobase Publishing

After the conclusion of the two Balkan wars, the landscape of the Balkan Peninsula changed dramatically: Serbia's size increased by 82 percent and Ottoman influence was eradicated from the region.

also conducted such a campaign of torture, maiming, and forced conversions of Muslim Albanians to Orthodoxy that more than 100,000 Albanians fled Kosovo for Bosnia. With the defeat of the Turks, Serbian national fervor boiled over—Kosovo had been recovered and the Battle of Kosovo Polje had been avenged. Bosnian Muslims, though, began to doubt the wisdom of a South Slav state.

Serbia's victory and expansion had an immediate impact on the region's artificial ethnic divisions. Serb enthusiasm, Bosnian

THE BLACK HAND

One day in June 1914, Gavrilo Princip waited on a street corner for a chance to murder the heir to the Habsburg throne. Princip was a trained assassin and leading member of an organization called *Ujedinjenje ili Smrt* (Union or Death), also known as the Black Hand. It was a secret Serbian organization formed in 1911 to conduct terrorist actions against Austria. The professed goal of the Black Hand was to end the arbitrary borders created by the European powers and to create a Greater Serbia by use of violence, if necessary. The Black Hand trained guerrilla fighters and assassins and arranged political murders.

Because of its highly secretive nature, the Black Hand had an elaborate initiation ceremony. Men wearing masks and hooded cloaks would swear in new members at a table draped in a black cloth. Upon the table lay a cross, a dagger, and a revolver. Initiates had to stand at the table and recite the following oath:

I [state your name], becoming a member of the organization Ujedinjenje ili Smrt, swear by the sun which is shining on me, by the earth which is feeding me, by God, by the blood of my ancestors, by my honor and my life, that from this moment until my death I will serve faithfully the cause of this organization and will always be ready to undergo any sacrifices for it. I swear by God, by honor of my life, that I will carry out all orders and commands unconditionally. I swear by God, honor and life, that I shall take to the grave all secrets of this organization. May God and my comrades in this organization judge me, if intentionally or unintentionally, I break or fail to observe this act of allegiance.*

Muslim anxiety, and divided Croat public opinion disrupted the relatively peaceful relations between the three major ethnic groups of a future Yugoslav state. Incendiary Serb celebrations in Sarajevo and other Bosnian towns over the Serbs' victories moved Bosnian Muslim leaders to side with Habsburg authorities in opposing Serb rule in Kosovo. Some Bosnian Croats joined those Serbs, calling for a new Yugoslav state to displace Habsburg rule. Others opposed Serb rule, siding with the Muslims.

By 1914, the Black Hand had several hundred members, perhaps as many as 2,500. Black Hand members often held important army and government positions, and many were Serbian military officers. The leader, Colonel Dragutin Dimitrljevic, was head of military intelligence of the Serbian Army and always went by his code name, Apis. Indeed, it was Apis who decided that Archduke Franz Ferdinand should die.

Of the seven assassins in Sarajevo that day, Princip was the one who succeeded in killing Ferdinand and his wife, Sophie. Because of the careful secrecy of the Black Hand, it was not found out to be the instigator of the crime until many weeks later. By that time, guilt for the murder had settled on Princip in particular and Serbia in general. Tensions between Serbia and Austria eventually drew the other European powers into a world war.

Gavrilo Princip was not sentenced to death at his trial because he was just under the legal age at which he could be executed. He died in an Austrian prison of tuberculosis after enduring years of solitary confinement and brutal conditions. Although he acted with the help of the Black Hand, whose goal was the formation of Greater Serbia, he denied killing the Archduke in the name of Serbia. At his trial he said, "I am a Yugoslav nationalist, aiming for the unification of all Yugoslavs, and I do not care what form of state, but it must be free of Austria."**

---

*   As quoted in Tim Judah, *The Serbs: History, Myth, and the Destruction of Yugoslavia.* New Haven, Conn.: Yale University Press, 1997, p. 96.

** Ibid., 97.

Such was the unsettled situation when Archduke Franz Ferdinand scheduled his ill-timed tour of Sarajevo on the anniversary of the Battle of Kosovo Polje, June 28, 1914. The Archduke knew that his first official visit to Sarajevo was fraught with danger. Since the annexation of Bosnia-Herzegovina, Sarajevo had become a hotbed of Serbian nationalism. Even though Ferdinand claimed to favor autonomy for the two provinces, Serbs hated the Habsburg Dynasty and the Austro-Hungarian Empire that Ferdinand represented.

It was a warm and sunny June morning when Ferdinand's procession wound through the narrow streets of Sarajevo. Ferdinand, his wife, and the governor of Bosnia riding together in an open car passed seven assassins armed with bombs and revolvers. All the would-be assassins were Bosnian students working in conjunction with a secret Serbian nationalist society called the Black Hand. The first would-be assassin did nothing, but the next man threw his bomb into the car. It bounced off Ferdinand's arm and exploded near another vehicle, wounding many. For various reasons, the remaining would-be assassins failed at their mission.

Later that day, as Ferdinand, his wife, and the governor headed toward the hospital to visit the people who had been wounded in the bomb attack, Gavrilo Princip, the last assassin, fired his revolver into the car. Both shots found their mark—the heir to the Habsburg throne and his wife died shortly thereafter.

The assassination brought to a head tensions between Serbia and the Austro-Hungarian Empire. As other European powers took sides, international conflict seemed imminent. Convinced that the assassination had been plotted within the Serbian government, the Habsburg leaders felt that they would have to act decisively. Within a month, Austria declared war on Serbia. Nationalist aspirations and international rivalries transformed that conflict into first a European war and ultimately a worldwide struggle, involving 60 nations. This global conflagration would destroy many old arbitrary borders and create new ones.

6

The First
Yugoslavia

No event in modern history played a greater role in redrawing arbitrary global borders than World War I. The Great War marked the beginning of the end of European global dominance. The end of the war ushered in a period of state building for many areas of the globe and greater political freedoms for formerly colonized peoples. By the end of the war, the Habsburg Empire, the Russian Empire, the German Empire, and the Ottoman Empire

THE PARIS PEACE CONFERENCE AND VERSAILLES SETTLEMENT

World War I destroyed the arbitrary borders of the traditional European empires and made possible the establishment of a new order in the Balkan Peninsula, and indeed the world over. The war lasted four years and three months and involved 60 sovereign states. By the end of the war, four great empires disappeared: the German, Russian, Turkish, and Austro-Hungarian. Restoring order and drawing new borders proved quite difficult amid such turmoil. Officially, the war ended in 1918, but hostilities continued for another five years.

Eventually, the fighting ceased, and a peace had to be established. Although representatives of 32 states attended the peace conference held in Paris in January 1919 to write the peace treaties, three men dominated the proceedings: Woodrow Wilson, president of the United States; Georges Clemenceau, prime minister of France; and Lloyd George, prime minister of Great Britain. These became known as the Big Three, because they made most of the decisions at the conference.

The conference resulted in the signing of five treaties: The Treaty of Versailles with Germany, The Treaty of Saint-Germain with Austria, the Treaty of Trianon with Hungary, the Treaty of Neuilly with Bulgaria, and the Treaty of Sèvres with Turkey. Together, these treaties ended the old European global order and created new nations along arbitrary borders.

Before the conference opened in 1919, both the Russian and Austro-Hungarian empires collapsed, and new states emerged along arbitrary borders. The Big Three, therefore, had to accept the existence ceased to exist, and all the old ruling dynasties of Europe lay in ruin. In its wake, the war left ghastly human casualties, severely damaged national economies, and discredited cultural traditions. With the destruction of four empires, World War I also saw the creation of several new nations struggling to establish and maintain social and political borders. The new Kingdom of Serbs, Croats, and Slovenes—later renamed Yugoslavia—was one of these.

of the new states of Yugoslavia, Czechoslovakia, Estonia, Latvia, Lithuania, and Poland when crafting territorial settlements after the war.

The Treaty of Versailles, signed with Germany on June 28, 1919, is perhaps the most important and well known of these treaties. It reflected two basic ideas that governed all the Paris negotiations and the Versailles settlement: punishment of the defeated and the maintenance of the principle of self-determination. The Treaty of Versailles assigned guilt for the war to Germany and demanded reparations. Indeed, Germany paid a heavy price for its defeat.

Taken together, the treaties greatly altered the arbitrary borders on the Balkans. The Treaty of Saint-Germain similarly meted out severe punishment to Austria: The country lost Bosnia, Herzegovina, and Dalmatia to the newly created Yugoslav state. Under the Treaty of Trianon, Yugoslavia also gained the territory of Croatia from Hungary. Finally, the Treaty of Neuilly forced Bulgaria to give western Macedonia to Yugoslavia.

These changes in arbitrary borders in the Balkans had a tremendous impact. Yugoslavia went from encompassing 33,891 square miles in 1914 to 96,134 square miles in 1923. Consequently, the population jumped from 4,548,000 to 12,017,000, nearly tripling in size.* Serbia gained the most on a percentage basis, more than tripling in size and population. Yugoslavia faced serious problems as a result of its expanded borders, including friction between the majority Serbs and minority Croats over the form of government Yugoslavia should adopt. These questions were never fully resolved and, in less than 25 years, a new war would disrupt the region.

* J. A. Lukacs, *The Great Powers and Eastern Europe.* New York: American Book Company, 1953, pp. 32–33.

Nikola Pašić, who served as Serbian premier from 1903 to 1926, was an advocate of Serbian national unity. After a united Yugoslavia was established in 1918, he headed Serbia's strongest political group, the Radical Party, which promoted Serbian interests above those of a greater Yugoslavia.

During the war, various groups exerted great pressure to unite the South Slavs of Europe—the Serbs, Croats, and Slovenes. They aimed to form a nation based on "Brotherhood and Unity." At first glance, this would seem appropriate because all three groups were descendents of Slavic tribes that settled in southeastern Europe. As we have seen, however, arbitrary borders separated these ethnic groups throughout history. They share no one universal language or religion. Serbs are Orthodox, whereas Slovenes and Croats are strict Roman Catholic and many Bosnians are Muslim. Serbs use both the Cyrillic and Latin alphabet, but Croats use only the Latin one. The Slovenian language, although considered Slavic, is vastly different from Serbo-Croatian. Despite these deep divisions, many intellectuals and politicians sought to form a new kingdom that would unite the South Slavs.

With the end of World War I and the collapse of the Austro-Hungarian and Ottoman empires, the conditions were right for proclaiming a new kingdom of Serbs, Croats, and Slovenes. Even before the war ended, three organizations became very active in promoting the idea of a South Slav state: the Serbian government, the Yugoslav Committee, and the Zagreb National Council.

During the war, in 1915, the combined armies of Germany, Austria, and Bulgaria overran Serbia. Serbian forces trekked through the winter snows of Kosovo and Albania to reach Corfu, where a Serbian government-in-exile was established. Prince-Regent Alexander Karageorgevic' headed this government, with Nikola Pašic' continuing as premier. War losses placed the Serbian leaders in an extremely weak position—during the war, 40 percent of Serbian armed forces, or 275,000 men, and 25 percent of the total population had died.[17] Nonetheless, Pašic' and most of his colleagues thought primarily in terms of furthering Serbian national unity. They wanted postwar Serbia to include Bosnia-Herzegovina as a centralized Orthodox state under the Karageorgevic' Dynasty. Despite the fact that, before the war, Serbian intellectuals and students had been in the forefront of advocating a united South Slav state, the government-in-exile rejected the notion.

At the same time, Croatian and Slovenian leaders held a different position. Several members of the 1905 Serb-Croat Coalition organized a group of powerful and energetic Croatian émigrés into the Yugoslav Committee. It aimed to create a South Slav state composed primarily of Croats and Slovenes.

Despite many contradictions in their attitudes toward South Slav unification, events forced Pašić and the Yugoslav Committee to come to an understanding. They met in Corfu in June and July 1917[18] and decided that the Serbian government and the Yugoslav Committee would cooperate to establish a Yugoslav state. The new state would be a constitutional monarchy ruled from Belgrade, the Serbian capital, under the Karageorgevic Dynasty. Pašić and the Yugoslav Committee made these decisions official in July 1917 in the Declaration of Corfu.

Some Croats approved of the Declaration of Corfu. In an action resembling those taken by the Yugoslav Committee and the Serbian government, a powerful group of men in Zagreb created the National Council of Slovenes, Croats, and Serbs in October 1918. This organization, with a Slovene president and Serb and Croat vice presidents, declared its support for the establishment of a democratic South Slav state. Working closely with the Yugoslav Committee, the National Council met with the Serbian government to propose a unified Yugoslavia. Prince Alexander accepted the proposal and on December 1, 1918, the Kingdom of the Serbs, Croats, and Slovenes was born.

Conflict arose at once. By all accounts, the most important question concerned the form the new Yugoslavia should take: Should it be organized as a centralized state or should it adopt a federal structure? It is little wonder that this issue was contentious in view of the disparate origins and composition of the state. The new Yugoslavia consisted of Slovenia and Dalmatia, former territories of Austria; Croatia-Slavonia, formerly autonomous regions of Hungary; Bosnia-Herzegovina, Austro-Hungarian provinces administered jointly by their ministry of finance; and Montenegro and Serbia, former independent kingdoms that included portions of Macedonia and the Turkish territories.

Given this background, it is understandable why the leaders of Yugoslavia met with so much difficulty in their attempts to construct a viable state. Their efforts eventually failed, as is indicated by the stormy course of Yugoslavia in the interwar period.

The leaders of the new state immediately sought to establish a constituent assembly that was to be elected on the basis of universal male suffrage. The constituent assembly then would draft a constitution. Under the best of circumstances, it would have been difficult to merge ethnicities with such vastly different historic, social, and religious experiences. Yet in the new Yugoslavia, the lines of conflict had existed along arbitrary borders for centuries. Representatives of the various political factions quarreled about the drawing of electoral districts. They fought over the basis of political representation. They argued over how to proceed. All the old political parties remained in existence, and new ones appeared, representing a myriad of interests and opinions. Indeed, as many as 40 political parties participated in the first elections.[19]

Not surprisingly, the new state did not represent an equal partnership, even though the first Yugoslav government, founded in January 1919, incorporated many groups. Regent Alexander of Serbia was to be the king. A Serb, Stojan Protić, was the premier, and there was to be a Slovenian vice premier. The minister of foreign affairs was a Dalmatian, and the national council had Serb and Montenegrin representatives.

Despite tremendous difficulties, the election proceeded, and the Yugoslavs elected a constituent assembly in November 1920. The election was fair and free, which made it an anomaly in Yugoslav politics. Nonetheless, from the very beginning, various aspects of the political situation made disintegration more likely than unity. The distinct regions that comprise Yugoslavia had experienced drastically different levels of economic development. Legal traditions within different areas also differed greatly. Nearly all parties within the new government disagreed over the critical issue of whether the state should be centralized or a decentralized federation.

The two most important parties represented in the constituent assembly were the Serbian Radical Party and the Croatian People's Peasant Party (CPPP). Nikola Pašić, the former premier of the Serbian government-in-exile in Corfu during World War I, headed the Radical Party. The Radical Party, founded in 1881, was the strongest political party in Serbia. Being staunchly nationalistic, it vehemently advanced a procentrist agenda and advocated for a Greater Serbia.

The CPPP was the antithesis of the Radical Party. Organized in 1904 by Stjepan and Ante Radic´, the CPPP had the overwhelming support of the Croatian people. Stjepan Radic´ headed it until he was murdered in 1928. In opposition to the Serbian Radical Party, the CPPP demanded a federal structure with full local government. Radic´ distrusted the Serb centralists. As a result, conflict erupted at every step between the Serb and Croat parties.

Despite the problems, on June 28, 1921, on St. Vitus Day and the anniversary of the Battle of Kosovo Polje, the constituent assembly adopted a new constitution, which became known as the Vidovdan (or St. Vitus Day) Constitution. It was a centralist document based on the prewar Serbian constitution. It provided for a one-chamber parliament and a centralized administrative system. According to the new constitution, the king controlled the army, and the government had virtually unlimited power to use the police and militia.

Unfortunately, the constitution caused more problems than it solved. It described Serbs, Croats, and Slovenes as "three tribes" of the same nation.[20] It did not, however, recognize Macedonians, Montenegrins, or Muslims as being separate tribes with political rights, and it ignored the Albanians in Kosovo altogether. Further, because of manipulation by Serb politicians, a simple majority of the constituent assembly and not the specified two-thirds majority passed into the text of the constitution. Because Serbs comprised a majority, this provision gave the Serbs an undue advantage. Slovenian and Croat representatives bitterly objected to the resultant Serb domination over other Yugoslav nationalities.[21] The principle of "one man, one vote" as promised by the constitution allowed for the largest nation—Serbia—to control the others.

Compounding the political problems facing the new nation, uneven economic and social borders presented tremendous obstacles to Yugoslav unity. In 1921, nearly 80 percent of the population engaged in agriculture as their main occupation, but Yugoslav agriculture was in a state of chronic crisis. Small landholdings barely provided subsistence for the peasants. Over time, the situation got worse. By 1931, two-thirds of farming households in Yugoslavia owned less than 12.5 acres (5 hectares) of land, and 700,000 families owned less than 5 acres (2 hectares).[22] Generally, land distribution tended toward smaller and smaller land holdings, with less and less efficient productivity. Rural overpopulation and a low level of technology intensified this low productivity. The result was widespread rural poverty.

In addition, industrial development was slow and unequally distributed throughout Yugoslavia. The lands under Habsburg rule developed the lion's share of industry. Moreover, the new state inherited four different railroad systems, seven different bodies of law, and several different currencies.[23] Merging these multiple systems took great time and effort and was fraught with problems. Tremendous disparities in economic and political power exacerbated these problems. For example, Serbia, which was largely agrarian, accounted for only 25 percent of Yugoslav revenues, but its representatives made up four-fifths of government personnel.[24]

Serbian centralism emanating from Belgrade dominated Yugoslav politics. Serbs controlled the main ministries and the armed forces; they held the most important diplomatic posts and headed the four most important banking institutions—the National Bank, State Mortgage Bank, the Postal Savings Bank, and the Agricultural Bank. Serbian rule rested on King Alexander's complete control of the army, as granted by the constitution, and his right to convene and disband the parliament at any time and for any reason. These extraordinary powers ensured that arbitrary borders would serve Serb ends and prohibited any opposition parties to act in concert against Serb

In June 1928, Puniša Račić, a member of the Serb Radical Party, assassinated CPPP leader Stjepan Radić in the Yugoslavian parliament building in Belgrade. In addition to Radić, who became a martyr for the Croatians, four other Croatian deputies were shot by Račić.

domination. This domination kept the parliament in a state of chaos.

A critical turning point in Yugoslav politics came in 1928. In the midst of escalating tensions between Serb centralists and Croat federalists, a wild crime on June 20 brought an end to

Yugoslav democracy. On that day, Puñisa Račić, a Montenegrin deputy of the Serb Radical Party, entered a session of Parliament, pulled a revolver out of his overcoat, and began firing on the Croatian deputies. Two died instantly and three others were wounded. One of the wounded was Stjepan Radić, the popular leader of the CPPP. He died a few weeks later from wounds sustained in the shooting. The Croatian cause now had a martyr. Radić's death not only radicalized the Croatian nationalist movement, but it also created an unbridgeable barrier between Serbs and Croats.

Croatian peasants responded to the death of their leader with rioting and a call for a free and independent Croatia. Croatian members of the parliament left Belgrade for home, vowing to have nothing to do with the "bloody" parliament until they could create a new federal Yugoslavia. On February 4–5, 1929, King Alexander granted an audience to Radić's successor, Vladimir Maček. Maček demanded a new constitution that would reorganize the state into five federal units and limit the authority of the federal government to the army, foreign affairs, customs duties, and currency. King Alexander asked Serbian Radical Party leaders if they would go along with such a drastic reorganization. They responded with a resounding "No!"

King Alexander used this crisis to carry out a coup d'état (a violent takeover of the government). He issued a decree on January 6, 1929, that suspended the 1921 constitution and abolished the parliament. Later in the month, he outlawed all political parties and established his personal dictatorship. He justified these moves by claiming that they were in the interest of peace and order in the country. In fact, it was the king's last-ditch effort to preserve a Serb-dominated centralist regime.

On September 3, 1931, King Alexander issued a new constitution that remained in place until the Nazi invasion in 1941. This new constitution was merely window dressing for the royal dictatorship, which operated as before. It established a centralized police state with strict censorship, serious curtailment of civil liberties, and severe penalties for any actions furthering separatism.

Alexander hoped he could create by force a Yugoslav nationalism to replace the particularism of the past. With this aim in mind, he changed the name of the country from the Kingdom of the Serbs, Croats, and Slovenes to the Kingdom of Yugoslavia. Unfortunately, it would take much more than a new name and a new constitution to create the desired national unity—the arbitrary borders were much too divisive.

Following the adoption of the new constitution, Croats remained faithful to the memory of their martyred leader, Stjepan Radić, and continued to vote for members of the CPPP despite electoral shenanigans and police intimidation. Consequently, the national dictatorship that Alexander hoped would foster national unity became in practice an anti-Croatian dictatorship.

King Alexander knew that his dictatorship failed to unite the country and that Yugoslav nationalism was a myth. Serbo-Croatian hatred remained as strong as ever. Some say that the king intended to end the dictatorship and replace it with a more representative government. If this is so, he did not have the opportunity. On October 9, 1934, Croatian and Macedonian extremists, with the help of Italian and Hungarian authorities, assassinated him in Marseilles, France.[25]

Along with King Alexander was buried all hope of a monarchial Yugoslavia. At the same time, his death won for him the honored place as a symbol of national unity that he could not achieve in life. The genuine mourning expressed throughout the country, even in Croatia, and the uncertainty of what would come next produced a mood of cautious compromise in the government. For a brief moment of national solidarity, the Serbs had a chance to offer some conciliatory gesture to the Croats, but unfortunately they let the moment pass. Alexander's death brought about a regrouping of political forces, but they were in a race against time.

Alexander's death also intensified Croatian demands for independence and threatened the Yugoslav government with new crises. Finally, in August 1939, the Serbs and Croats signed an agreement that radically altered the new constitution and reordered the Kingdom of Yugoslavia. More important, the agreement granted Croatia autonomous status through the creation of a specific Croatian territory and a separate government organization. Even though Croatia remained subordinate to the central Yugoslav government and the new regent, Prince Paul, the agreement held out the possibility of a federal Yugoslavia, rather than a Serb-dominated centralized state.

Unfortunately, as was often the case in Yugoslav politics, the 1939 agreement was inadequate and caused even more problems. Croat politicians remained angry because their autonomy was limited. Serb politicians became angry because of the loss of their dominion and the move away from centralism. Nonetheless, the agreement was a first step in revising Yugoslavia's national foundations, problematic as it was.

Finally, the rise of Fascist Germany and Benito Mussolini's Italy would spell doom for the first Yugoslavia. On April 6, 1941, the Nazi *Luftwaffe* (Air Force) attacked Belgrade. Only 18 months after Serbs and Croats signed their 1939 agreement, Yugoslavia collapsed under foreign invasion. Adolf Hitler and Benito Mussolini split Yugoslavia between Germany and Italy, with some territory parceled out to Bulgaria and Hungary. Yet again, foreign powers created new arbitrary borders. Thus, the Kingdom of Yugoslavia would die as it had been born—amidst the destructive forces of war.

7

World War and the Destruction of the First Yugoslavia

On April 6, 1941, Adolf Hitler's air force, the Luftwaffe, leveled Belgrade, inflicting horrendous casualties upon the civilian population. World War II had come to Yugoslavia. In less than two weeks, the Germans swept without resistance over all of Yugoslavia and down to the southern capes of Greece. The Yugoslav Army surrendered, and King Peter II fled. Consequently, the country fell under the control of Hitler and Mussolini, who dismembered the Kingdom of Yugoslavia. The German and Italian occupying forces set up arbitrary social divisions between ethnicities that inflamed nationalistic hatreds. Once again, foreign powers laid out new arbitrary borders, with disastrous results for the future of the South Slav peoples.

The collapse of Yugoslavia was rapid. Although, within days, some 375,000 soldiers and officers became POWs (prisoners of war) under the Axis powers (Nazi Germany, Fascist Italy, and Imperial Japan), many hundreds of thousands did not.[26] For the most part, members of the Yugoslav Army simply went home. The speed with which Yugoslavia collapsed meant, however, that Axis forces did not occupy most of Yugoslavia and had not disarmed the Yugoslav Army. This failure to occupy and disarm Yugoslavia would spell disaster for Hitler, as resistance movements emerged throughout the Balkans.

Having overrun Yugoslavia, the Axis powers immediately set about partitioning it. Slovenia was divided into two parts, with the northern end going to Germany and the southern end going to Italy. In the north, Germany adopted a harsh policy of denationalization, exiling Slovenian intellectuals and professionals and bringing in German settlers. Most of Macedonia went to Bulgaria, whereas Kosovo and the western part of Macedonia were given to Italian-controlled Albania. The Italians also occupied large portions of Bosnia and Herzegovina.

Only two small states with puppet governments, Serbia and Croatia, remained of what had been Yugoslavia. A pro-Axis force emerged to rule the ruins of Croatia. This party, the Ustasha, or Rebels, was an extremist, Fascist wing of the Croatian nationalist party. The Ustasha, with the patronage of Italy and Hungary, set up a puppet state, the "Independent State of Croatia" (NDH in its Croatian acronym), and installed Ante Pavelić as the *führer* (leader). The arbitrary borders of this new "independent" state extended eastward, to include most of Bosnia-Herzegovina. At the same time, Croatia lost much of the Dalmatian coast to the Italians.

Although the Ustasha never achieved mass support with Pavelić as führer, extremists ruled Independent Croatia and law and order rapidly disintegrated into chaos. The Ustasha enthusiastically followed the Nazi program of extermination of Jewish communities in Croatia and Bosnia-Herzegovina. On its own, the Ustasha began systematically arresting and killing Jews. Ultimately, 26,000 Yugoslav Jews perished in Croatian death camps.[27]

The vast majority of Croats were against such policies, but the Ustasha conducted its own program of brutal repression of Communists and all-out genocide against the Serbs living within the NDH. Svetozar Babić, a Serb living in the new Croatia who was 14 years old when Pavelić came to power, recalls:

> When the war began I remember the German troops passing through. There was no defense, no fighting, they just passed through. Then the Croats nationalized our shop and those of the other Serbs and Jews without any right to compensation. But there was no threat to anyone's life. Early in May they took away five or six Jewish families. We thought, "Okay, they are against the Jews, but we are Christians." We did not think they were against us. Then came the night of May 10–11. Ustashas, not locals, men with guns came knocking on doors at midnight asking who was in the house. They took my father and my brother. My mother lied and said I was twelve, which saved my life. They said it was for an investigation, and there was already a line of people outside on the street. On the next day we were allowed to bring food to the prisoners, but on the 13th they told us that

they [the prisoners] had all been taken to Germany to work.
A few days later we heard they had all been killed.[28]

This massacre was not the first, nor would it be the last. The
Ustasha turned Croatia into the main slaughterhouse of the war
in the Balkans. Of the 947,000 Yugoslavs who died during the
war, 530,000, or 62 percent, did so in the NDH. Of the estimated
192,000 Croats who died during the war, approximately 172,000
of them perished in the NDH. At the same time, about 300,000
Serbs, or roughly one in six of the total Serb population, died in
Croatia and Bosnia-Herzegovina.[29] This is largely because the
Ustasha adopted a policy of exterminating the Serbs much like
the Nazis had toward the Jews.

The Ustasha defined Croats as a pure Aryan race, whereas
they classed Serbs as racial enemies. Just as the Nazis forced the
Jews to wear yellow Stars of David, the Ustasha forced the Serbs
to wear armbands with the letter "P" for Pravoslavac, or
Orthodox. The Ustasha set up several concentration camps, then
they would usually sweep into a village or rural town at night.
They would slaughter Serbs in their homes, or round them up
and kill them in pits, forest clearings, or burning churches. Since
it would be impossible to kill all the Serbs, Pavelic decreed that
the survivors had to convert to Catholicism or be exiled.

The massacres were no secret—the Ustasha wanted to instill
fear into the Serb population. The Nazis and the Italians both
opposed this reign of terror against the Serbs. Indeed, the
Germans had hoped to install a friendly regime and exploit the
NDH for resources and men. The killing of thousands of men,
women, and children led to Serbian revolts. The Nazis feared
they would have to divert German troops away from the fronts
to control Serbian uprisings. In the Italian-controlled sections of
the NDH, the situation was a bit different. Horrified by the
atrocities, the Italian military extended protection to the Serbs
and ended up reoccupying areas that had been given over to the
NDH. Ordinary Italian soldiers aided the Serbs and protected
them from the Ustasha. In some cases, Italian military leaders

arrested leading members of the Ustasha and shot them. As one senior Italian military officer observed, the NDH should not be seen as an independent state, but rather as "a sick man who has brought himself to his own grave."[30]

During the war, Kosovo also erupted into chaos and terror. Following the collapse of Yugoslavia in 1941, most of Kosovo became part of the Italian-ruled greater Albania. As we have seen, Albanians occupied and claimed Kosovo after the Battle of Kosovo Polje in 1389. Then, following the First Balkan War in 1912, Serbs reclaimed the region and killed or drove out tens of thousands of Albanians. Consequently, both the Serbs and the Albanians saw Kosovo as their own.

When Italy declared Kosovo part of greater Albania in 1941, Kosovar Albanians immediately began organized massacres of the Serbs. So terrible were the massacres that the Italians often had to intervene. No one knows for sure how many Serbs died or fled. Some sources estimate that as many as 70,000 Serbs became refugees and 10,000 died.[31] One Italian commissioner in Kosovo at the time wrote in his memoirs that "the Albanians are out to exterminate the Serbs," and that in some villages, "not a single house has a roof: Everything has been burned down. . . . There are headless bodies of men and women strewn on the ground."[32]

Although the Italians controlled Kosovo and Croatia was (in theory) independent, Serbia came under the authority of the local German commander. The German attack itself inflicted far more physical damage on the Serbian capital of Belgrade than anywhere else in Yugoslavia. Two days of continuous bombing killed about 2,300 civilians in Belgrade alone.[33] After a week of authorized looting, the Nazis took complete control of all urban centers in Serbia. The Germans reduced the Serbian borders to those that had been established before the First Balkan War. To thwart any resistance movements, the Nazis attempted to rally some popular support for themselves by persuading the Serb General Milan Nedić to form "a Government of National Salvation."

Nedić had been the chief of staff of the Yugoslav Army before the German invasion. Unlike Pavelić, the Croatian Ustasha leader who shared Nazi ideology, Nedić had no ties to Fascism. Rather, he saw himself as the temporary representative of Yugoslavia's exiled king. Despite ideological differences, the Germans allowed him to form a small military force. They kept a close eye on the Nedić regime, though, and maintained careful control over the country.

By 1942, things looked bleak for all the Yugoslav peoples. The Axis had partitioned Yugoslavia, persecuted its populations, and purposefully inflamed nationalistic hatreds to the point of mass fratricidal butchery. Kosovar Albanians indiscriminately

During World War II, Germany established a puppet state in Serbia led by Milan Nedić, who was the chief of staff of the Yugoslav Army prior to the invasion. Pictured here are German tanks rolling into Belgrade on April 17, 1941, 11 days after the Luftwaffe, the German Air Force, killed thousands of the city's residents during a massive bombing operation.

massacred Serbs. The Croatian Ustasha slaughtered tens of thousands of Serbs, Jews, and Gypsies. Muslims joined in the bloodshed, linking forces with Catholics to wage war against Orthodox Serbs and Jews. Even some members of the Croatian Catholic hierarchy endorsed the massacres and participated in the forced conversions.

The Serbs, of course, retaliated whenever possible, exacting bloody revenge in Bosnia-Herzegovina and elsewhere.[34] Yugoslavia had become a place of death, destruction, and bloody disputes. Yet out of this hell emerged resistance movements that would unify and purify Yugoslavia.

Had Hitler not been in such a rush to invade the Soviet Union, things might have gone very differently for Yugoslavia. In May 1941, at the beginning of the German invasion and occupation, the Yugoslavs were in a state of shock. The Nazis had all but destroyed the Yugoslav Army, had routed the king, and had brutally torn the state to pieces. The Germans, though, not willing to take the time to finish the job in Yugoslavia, almost immediately turned against the Soviet Union, smashing across the Russian frontier on June 22, 1941. Code-named Operation Barbarossa, the invasion stretched along a 1,500-mile front and was the largest invading force in modern warfare.

Hitler did not take the time to mop up in the Balkans before launching Operation Barbarossa, because he was determined to conquer the Soviet Union before winter set in. Time did not allow the Germans to fully find and disarm the scattered Yugoslav Army units. Nor could Hitler afford to leave strong garrisons of German soldiers behind to control the Balkans, because he needed every available soldier for Operation Barbarossa. Consequently, within a few weeks after the occupation, a few bold leaders emerged to lead resistance movements against the Germans.

One such leader was Colonel Draža Mihailović, a regular army officer and ardent Serb nationalist. He fought in World War I, but he failed to get a promotion to general because of a drunken misadventure. When the Germans invaded, Mihailović was stationed in northern Bosnia. Refusing to accept the surrender, he trekked from Herzegovina to central Serbia with a small band of followers expecting to link up with the main lines of Yugoslav military resistance. He found none. So he went to an isolated area in western Serbia with only 26 men to build a resistance force.³⁵ In very little time, he had attracted some 10,000 followers who came to be known as the Chetniks.

Deriving the name from the guerrilla fighters who opposed Ottoman rule, Mihailovic′ himself chose the name Chetnik. A Chetnik was literally a member of a Cheta, or military detachment, who had fought against the Turks in the nineteenth century. The name surfaced again during World War I, especially among Bosnian Serb guerrillas. Mihailovic′'s Chetniks were largely nationalist—in other words, anti-Croat and anti-Communist. They adopted all the old symbols of the Serbian Empire, as well as a skull-and-crossbones flag with the slogan, "Freedom or Death."

Mihailovic′ presumably acted in coordination with the Yugoslav government-in-exile in London. His Chetniks took to the mountains in rebellion against the Nedic′ regime. Local leaders in various parts of Serbia organized Chetnik bands in the traditional fashion. Those under Mihailovic′'s command were well disciplined, but other bands in Bosnia, Herzegovina, Croatia, or Montenegro operated more or less independently.

The loose organization, lack of discipline, and strong Serbian nationalism prohibited Mihailovic′ from building up an efficient army. Moreover, the border between resistance and collaboration can be very blurry: Lacking the resources for a direct assault against the Axis powers, Mihailovic′ sometimes found himself cooperating with them for survival. At his trial in 1946 for war crimes and collaboration with the enemy, Mihailovic′ said, "Destiny was merciless with me when it threw me into the most difficult whirlwinds. I wanted much. I began much, but the whirlwind, the world whirlwind, carried me and my work away."³⁶

The other major resistance movement, the Partisans, differed greatly from the Chetniks. Josip Broz, popularly known as

Josip Broz Tito, pictured here in 1944, was the leader of the Yugoslav Partisans, who led a guerrilla campaign to liberate the country from Germany beginning in July 1941. After Yugoslavia was free from German rule in 1945, Tito served as premier and president of the country until his death in 1980.

Tito, led the Partisans. Half Croat, half Slovene, Tito served in the Austro-Hungarian Army during World War I and had been taken prisoner by the Russians. In 1917, when the Russian Empire collapsed in a Communist revolution led by the Bolsheviks, Tito sided with the Communists. Upon his return to Yugoslavia, Tito played a key role in the underground Communist movement, eventually becoming the head of the outlawed Yugoslav Communist Party.

When the Germans attacked the Soviet Union in June 1941, Joseph Stalin, the Communist leader of the Union of Soviet Socialist Republics (USSR), called for Communists to attack Nazis whenever and wherever possible. Responding to Stalin's

JOSIP BROZ TITO

Born on May 7, 1892, in a little Croatian village, Josip Broz Tito became the only premier of Yugoslavia to overcome divisive arbitrary borders and impose unity on the country. The son of a blacksmith, Tito was the seventh of 15 children born to Roman Catholic parents. At the age of 12, he left school for an apprenticeship and spent the next several years wandering the Austro-Hungarian Empire, working at various jobs. During World War I, he fought on the Russian front in the Austro-Hungarian Army and was captured by the Russians in 1915.

Within two years, revolution erupted in the Russian Empire, Tsar Nicholas II abdicated the throne, and Tito was released from prison. At the age of 18, Tito joined the Social Democratic Party, which strongly supported the Bolsheviks, and he headed to Petrograd to fight with the Russian revolutionaries. Again, tsarist troops captured and imprisoned him. When the Bolsheviks finally took power in October 1917, Tito was released from prison. He joined the Red Army and served with distinction in Russia's civil war, (1918–1920). Following the war, he returned to Croatia (now part of the newly formed Kingdom of Serbs, Croats, and Slovenes) and joined the Communist Party of Yugoslavia (CPY).

Between 1921 and the Nazi invasion of Yugoslavia in 1941, the Yugoslav government viewed Communism as a very dangerous political border and banned it. Consequently, Tito operated underground to organize and strengthen the CPY. He was arrested and imprisoned several times but continued to rise in the Communist Party ranks. After Germany attacked the Soviet Union in 1941, Tito became the military commander of the Partisans, issuing a call to arms with the slogan "Death to Fascism, Freedom to the People!"

Tito and the Partisans spent many years organizing and working underground, then led an effective resistance movement against the Nazis. They created a revolutionary government in areas liberated from Axis control. By war's end, Tito not only was the uncontested leader of Yugoslavia, but he also had the support of Russia and Britain.

As premier of Yugoslavia, Tito worked to weaken the rift between nationalities. He created a system that ensured equality among Yugoslavia's six republics. In the process, he greatly decentralized the federation, giving the republics a fair amount of autonomy. Tito also closed the breach between Communist and non-Communist countries by allowing a freer exchange of people and ideas than most Eastern bloc countries. Tito died on May 4, 1980, and within months, the arbitrary borders he had worked so hard to weaken began to reemerge.

call, Tito and the Partisans immediately began assaults against Germans in Serbia. They appealed to all parties and all nationalities for support. Using the idea of a popular front, the Partisans called for the unity of all patriotic forces against the foreign invaders. Eager to see action, the Chetniks joined with the Partisans to fight Germans. Within a few months, though, cooperation between the two resistance groups broke down, and Chetnik and Communist Partisan bands were soon killing each other.

One of the primary reasons for the bitter struggle between the two groups was a result of arbitrary political borders. The two groups had basic differences in their political outlooks. Mihailović, an officer in the king's army, regarded the Communists as lawless, atheistic criminals. Indeed, the first Yugoslavia legally banned all Communist parties. For their part, the Communists viewed the Chetniks as representatives of the bourgeois, imperialist, reactionary prewar regime that they had fought for years.

The heart of this struggle centered on what would come after the war—whether Yugoslavia should be restored as a monarchy, or whether a radically new Communist government should be formed.[37] In the end, Mihailović's Greater Serbian nationalism led to his defeat. Although the idea of a unified Serbia, free of Croats and Muslims, appealed to the conservative Serbian peasants, it was not an idea that most Yugoslav peoples could rally around. By contrast, the Partisans played down Communism in favor of the creation of a united Popular Front that appealed to far greater numbers of Yugoslavs. For example, in Bosnia, the Partisans' rallying cry was for a "free and brotherly Bosnia and Herzegovina in which the full equality of all Serbs, Croats, and Muslims will be ensured."[38]

The Chetniks and the Partisans also differed on what strategy should be used against the Axis. Mihailović feared that open attacks against the Germans would result in brutal reprisals. He was absolutely right: The Germans burned villages and began shooting 100 civilians for every German soldier killed.

Mihailović thought that resistance bands should lie low and not risk more reprisals until an Allied invasion could help them defeat the Germans. Tito's beliefs were diametrically opposed to Mihailović's. Tito believed that every German reprisal brought more people into the ranks of the Partisans. Consequently, the Partisans followed a path of uncompromising, continual resistance. In the end, these ideological borders proved too strong, and the two groups became bitter enemies engaged in open war with each other.

Despite brutal attacks by both the Germans and the Chetniks, the Partisans established a firm base for their resistance movement and by 1944 emerged as the clear masters of Yugoslavia. This is all the more impressive when one considers that, at the beginning of the occupation, the Communists of Yugoslavia were a small, illegal, and fiercely persecuted political party numbering fewer than 27,000.

A number of factors account for the stunning success of Tito and his Partisans. Their historic victory would be impossible to explain if they had relied on ideology alone. Instead, their appeal to the Yugoslav peoples lay in their patriotic, local, and democratic principles. They adopted the slogan "Death to Fascism, Freedom to the People," and they invited anyone who was willing to fight the enemy into their ranks. For example, in Slovenia, the Partisans allied themselves with the Christian Democrats. In Croatia, they recruited from the Croatian People's Peasant Party, as well as from Serbs who had suffered at the hands of the Ustasha. In Bosnia-Herzegovina, the Partisans brought together Jews, Muslims, Serbs, and Croats.

In short, the Partisans embraced arbitrary borders that unified, rather than divided, the Yugoslav peoples. At the same time, the Partisans never lost sight of their revolutionary goal. Tito knew full well that a Communist-led resistance movement would clear the way for postwar social change.

Another reason for the Communists' success was their use of National Liberation Committees as very effective instruments for expansion and administration. When they first occupied a town or village, Partisans would destroy the existing political structure by shooting the militia and civilian officials. They would burn police stations and all public records. Then they would set up a National Liberation Committee to act as a local government. In theory the local population elected these committees, but in practice they consisted of only local Partisans. In this way, the Partisans spread their influence throughout most of Yugoslavia.

Finally, during a war with all the worst abuses of ethnic and religious conflict, the Communists stayed steadfast to the principle of self-determination. Before the war had begun, the Communists had demonstrated a commitment to a federal Yugoslavia—to the principle of full equality for all peoples living in it. During the war, at a time when the renewal of Yugoslavia seemed absolutely impossible, the Communists offered a new vision of Yugoslavia expressed in the slogan "Brotherhood and Unity."

In 1943, more help came to the Partisans when Italy collapsed and the German position became more difficult. Huge quantities of Italian arms and ammunition fell into Partisan hands. Moreover, the growing conviction that the war would be won by the Allies led local leaders to side with the Partisans rather than the Germans.

By the end of the war, the Partisans established an advantage over any possible political opponent within Yugoslavia. From a small group committed to desperate actions against its occupiers, Tito's Partisans grew to become a force of 800,000 fighters. Tito ascribed the victory to Communist ideology. The real triumph, however, was that out of the bloodshed and destruction, the idea of a united Yugoslavia emerged. Once again the South Slavs looked to the future with hope. Intellectuals had created the first Yugoslavia. The new Yugoslavia that emerged after World War II was seen as a creation of the people. Out of this turmoil, a new basis of reconciliation and a new state with new arbitrary borders was forged.

8

The Second
Yugoslavia

As we have seen, the arbitrary borders of the first Yugoslavia collapsed after the invasion of Nazi Germany and the Axis allies just 23 years after it was founded. The disintegration was rapid and dramatic, and few people, in or out of Yugoslavia, believed it could be put back together again. Yet the impossible became probable under the leadership of Josep Broz Tito. Although Tito could not overcome centuries of arbitrary divisions that separated Serb from Croat, Bosnian from Slovene, and Catholic from Orthodox or Muslim, he could unite the South Slavs in a tenuous new Federal People's Republic of Yugoslavia that lasted until after his death.

The international environment following World War II was more favorable for the creation of a South Slav state than when the first Yugoslavia was created. The following exchange between Britain's prime minister Winston Churchill and one of his senior aides, Brigadier Fitzroy Maclean, reveals much about attitudes toward events in Yugoslavia at the time. As Maclean later recounts, after having told Churchill that Tito and the Partisans were openly and avowedly Communist and that after the war Yugoslavia would undoubtedly orient toward the Soviet Union,

> The Prime Minister's reply resolved my doubts:
> "Do you intend," he asked, "to make Yugoslavia your home after the war?"
> "No sir," I replied.
> "Neither do I," he said. "And, that being so, the less you and I worry about the form of Government they set up, the better. That is for them to decide. What interests us is, which of them is doing most harm to the Germans?"[39]

The Partisans' heroic survival, multiethnic composition, promised federal program, and uncompromising resistance to the enemy allowed Tito and the Communist Party of Yugoslavia to consolidate power. On November 19, 1943, the wartime Partisan parliament, known as the Anti-Fascist Council of the National Liberation of Yugoslavia, or AVNOJ, met in Bosnia and voted on a new Yugoslavia and a new set of arbitrary borders. In its final form, the new Yugoslavia would be a federation of six republics and two autonomous regions. The republics were Serbia, Croatia, Bosnia-Herzegovina, Montenegro, Macedonia, and Slovenia. The two autonomous regions, Kosovo and Vojvodina, would be a part of Serbia.

In reality, the shape of the new state would not be fully clear until the war ended. Tito, however, made one thing absolutely certain—a new Yugoslavia had to guarantee equality to all nationalities. The Partisans fought under the slogan of "Brotherhood and Unity," and they intended to craft a state from the same principles.

The Partisan parliament drew up most of the republic's boundaries, taking ethnic, historic, and economic borders into consideration. There were a few disputes, but overall, republic leaders did not contest the divisions. This was not because by some happy miracle everyone put aside old feuds. Rather, Tito made it clear that he would tolerate no opposition. Besides, leaders generally thought that the borders did not matter much because they were not dividing independent states, but regions within Yugoslavia.[40]

By the spring of 1945, all the enemy armies had left Yugoslavia, but the Partisans still faced internal opposition. The Tito regime made its first priority the defeat of any domestic forces that opposed it, along with finding and punishing pro-Axis war criminals and non-Fascist nationalistic opponents. The Chetnik forces, still loyal to the prewar regime and the idea of a Greater Serbia, were not terribly troublesome. By the end of the war, they numbered fewer than 12,000. The Partisans subsequently caught and killed most of them.[41] In 1946, the Partisans eventually captured, tried, and executed Mihailović, the leader of the Chetniks. The most brutal reprisals, however, were directed against the Croat supporters of the Pavelić regime and his Ustasha.

As the war drew to a close, and it became clear that Tito would dominate postwar Yugoslavia, the majority of Croats rushed to join the ranks of the victorious Partisans. Many

Draža Mihailović was the leader of the Chetniks—a Serbian nationalist group that supported the exiled royal government—who initially fought the Nazis during World War II but eventually turned their attention to the Partisans. After the war, many Chetniks, including Mihailović, who is pictured here during his trial in 1946, were accused of treason and executed.

thousands of Croats were not able to do so, though, because they had been members of the Ustasha or had openly opposed the Partisans' political stand. More than 100,000 of these people, together with their families, fled northward to turn themselves in to the British forces stationed there. They hoped that the British would protect them from retribution. Unfortunately, the Allies had already signed an agreement that all prisoners were to be turned over to the government against which they had fought. Consequently, the British handed these people over to the Partisans. What followed was to be the last wartime mass atrocity, as the Partisans killed between 40,000 and 100,000 suspected Ustasha and their supporters, including thousands of civilians.[42]

Indeed, the Tito regime used harsh measures to unify the South Slavs. He treated any expression of separatism or nationalism as a serious crime, and the coercion seemed to work. For a time, it appeared that all the old arbitrary borders that had caused so much suffering and bloodshed simply disappeared. Within two years, anyone could travel safely from one end of the country to the other, regardless of nationality, language, or religion. In a country where one-tenth of the population had either lost their lives fighting the enemy or were murdered in genocidal atrocities, this seemed miraculous. One reason for the surface calm in Yugoslavia was the strength of the Communist Party. Indeed, the Yugoslav Communist regime was in the best position of all the socialist governments in Eastern Europe at war's end. The Partisan forces, numbering more than 800,000, clearly controlled Yugoslavia. The new state also used police pressure, informers, and spies to destroy any political or nationalistic opposition.

Moreover, because of some stunning economic successes, the regime initially enjoyed broad popular support. At war's end, Yugoslavia was in dire shape. More than one million people had died, and the ravages of war inflicted tremendous physical damage, especially to the infrastructure. All rail lines and roads needed repair, rolling stock and repair facilities had been cut by one-half, and there were virtually no motor vehicles. Fifteen percent of prewar housing had been demolished, as had 40 percent of industrial enterprises. More than half of all livestock and agricultural machinery had been destroyed or damaged. Masses of people faced starvation if relief supplies did not reach them quickly.[43]

Despite all the destruction, Yugoslavia experienced a remarkable recovery. The country rapidly rebuilt rail and road networks. It opened ports to receive imports. By 1947, agricultural production recovered to prewar levels, and most industrial enterprises and mines resumed operation. Nowhere else in Eastern Europe had economic recovery been so rapid.

Communist-organized youth brigades conducted most of the recovery work. Young Communist leaders, often Partisan veterans, mobilized local youths into work groups, either by persuasion or coercion. Concentration camp prisoners formed separate brigades. Moreover, Yugoslavia received more aid from the United Nations Relief and Rehabilitation Agency (UNRRA) than any other country—$415 million.[44] This aid took the form of shipments of food, clothing, and medical supplies, as well as equipment to rebuild agriculture and industry.

The party also used propaganda to rally popular support around the ideology of Yugoslavism over socialism or federalism. Tito's Yugoslavia emphasized the unifying struggle against a common enemy and created the myth that the wartime success was attributable to a resolution of ethnic differences. In fact, the 1946 Yugoslav Constitution enshrined the principle of a single Yugoslavia, giving all peoples and republics equal rights and duties. In all quarters of Yugoslavia, the first postwar generation was eager to believe this propaganda and reject the arbitrary ethnic borders that promoted the ethnic cleansing that had taken more lives than the Nazis had.

Although the new Yugoslavia strongly affirmed the principle of national equality, the arbitrary sociopolitical and economic borders were less clear. Tito and the Communist leadership conjured up a romanticized picture of a Communist system. The educated elite, who supported Tito both during and after the war, failed to grasp the complexity of constructing a totally new economy, social structure, and political institutions. Their ideas went no further than some vague idealized Soviet model. Because Tito and his closest aides had visited the Soviet Union many times and had worked closely with the Comintern (the Moscow-based Communist International), they saw the difficulties the Soviet Union had in creating a new socialist order after the 1917 Communist revolution. Tito believed Yugoslavia could avoid the mistakes made by the Soviet Communists. He also thought, naively, that the Soviet Union would do everything in its power to help Yugoslavia.

Despite Yugoslav enthusiasm for all things Soviet, problems arose almost at once between the USSR and Yugoslavia. At war's end, the Soviet Red Army crossed the northern part of Yugoslavia, raising havoc as it went. On its passage, Soviet troops committed numerous crimes, including 111 which involved rape and murder. When Yugoslav authorities protested to Stalin, he dismissed these charges, commenting that after years of fighting, a Russian soldier should be expected to have "some fun with a woman."[45]

Another source of friction was the growing belief among Yugoslav leaders that the Soviet Union would not support Yugoslavia's international aims. They were particularly disturbed by reports that the three great wartime allies, Great Britain, the United States, and the USSR, intended to divide the Balkans into spheres of influence. Tito had an uneasy feeling that the country once again would be the victim of great power meddling. Moreover, the Soviet Union did very little to aid Yugoslavia's economic recovery. Indeed, Stalin seemed more intent on preventing the rise of a potential economic rival than aiding Yugoslavia's economic development.

Even though friction existed between Stalin and Tito before the war ended, tensions did not reach a boiling point until 1948. Tito, while steadfastly loyal to Communism and the Soviet state, had no intention of blindly obeying orders from Stalin. Further, Tito resented what he considered attempts by the Soviet Union to economically exploit Yugoslavia. Consequently, Tito and the Yugoslav leadership began making economic and foreign policy decisions without consulting Stalin. For his part, Stalin resented what he saw as the excessive self-confidence of the Yugoslavs. Stalin expected Tito, and all foreign Communists, to be reverent, not proud and independent.

By the beginning of 1948, relations between the Soviet Union and Yugoslavia devolved into a state of crisis. The main issue facing Tito was whether Yugoslavia would maintain independence or kowtow to the USSR. A terse correspondence between Stalin and Tito ensued, followed by threats, accusations, and denials. In the end, on June 28, 1948, the Communist bloc countries, under pressure from Stalin, voted to expel Yugoslavia from the Cominform (the Communist Information Bureau, which had been created to replace the Comintern).

Stalin chose this date with the intention of intimidating Tito. More predictably, though, choosing June 28, the anniversary of the Battle of Kosovo Polje in 1389, the date of the assassination of Franz Ferdinand in 1914, and the date of the proclamation of the first Yugoslav Constitution in 1921, had the opposite effect. It only posed a dramatic challenge to Tito. Tito emerged from this confrontation as a hero to all Yugoslavs and unquestionably the most revered figure in Yugoslav history.

THE TITO-STALIN SPLIT OF 1948

At the end of World War II, the Soviet Union's Red Army liberated most of Eastern Europe from Fascist control. Consequently, Stalin believed he had earned the right to influence or control the establishment of Communist regimes throughout the area. He ran into problems, however, when he came up against Tito in Yugoslavia.

Tito and the Partisans came to power during the war with no help from Stalin and with no backing by Russian troops. Moreover, as the Red Army passed briefly through Yugoslavia toward the end of the war, Russian soldiers committed theft, rape, and murder. Yugoslavs were understandably quite upset. After the war, when Soviet political and economic experts arrived in Belgrade to set up joint Soviet-Yugoslav industries, Yugoslavs criticized it as economic exploitation and political meddling. Perhaps more important, Tito had an ego the size of Stalin's.

Stalin had no desire to treat Tito as an equal, or allow him to become head of a Balkan Communist federation, but Tito would accept nothing less. So in February 1948, when Stalin proposed a federation that would join Yugoslavia and Bulgaria, and insisted that both countries must secure Moscow's approval for any foreign policy decisions, Tito balked. Unable to tolerate any kind of resistance, Stalin then invited members of the Yugoslav Communist Party to overthrow Tito. No one took up the challenge.

Confident that his political position was secure, Tito openly denounced Stalin and his policy of subordinating small socialist countries to the Soviet

Moreover, since Tito refused to capitulate, arbitrary borders not only divided the world between Communists and capitalists, there were now internal divisions within the Communist world as well.

Following the Tito-Stalin split, the Yugoslav regime rededicated itself to creating Soviet-style socialism. For example, in the late 1940s, Tito nationalized all private businesses, collectivized agriculture, and forced peasants to sell their produce at state-mandated prices. Tito had broken with Stalin but not with his political methods. The rigid Stalinist conception of state and

Union. Stalin responded by kicking Yugoslavia out of the socialist camp. Stalin then imposed economic boycotts and sanctions against Yugoslavia but stopped short of invading the country.

Yugoslavia's arbitrary geographic borders proved quite advantageous when Stalin forced Yugoslavia out of the Moscow-dominated Communist world: The country was located far enough away from the Soviet Union to escape invasion yet was close enough to Western capitalistic nations to receive aid not available to other Balkan countries. By combining ongoing criticism of Stalin and courting Western economic support, Tito secured enough Western loans and contracts to fare much better than most other Communist countries.

The Tito-Stalin split helped to weaken the arbitrary border between East and West during the cold war. Because of Tito, Yugoslavia's people enjoyed more freedoms than those in any other Eastern bloc country. Western tourists vacationed in Yugoslavia, and Tito promoted scientific exchanges with the West. At the same time, the Tito-Stalin split created an arbitrary division within the Communist world: Tito's Yugoslavia was clearly a Communist state, yet it was not a puppet state of the Soviet Union. Tito advocated different paths to socialism, whereas the Soviet Union tried to force all Communist countries under the control of Moscow. After his death in 1980, Tito was hailed as a hero—the David who defied the Russian Goliath.

NATO and Warsaw Pact Countries, 1955

Yugoslavia bordered several Eastern bloc countries, including Bulgaria and Romania, but it was never part of the Soviet-controlled countries that made up the Warsaw Pact.

society prevailed among Tito and the ruling elite, and if repressive Stalinist measures were needed to accomplish these goals, then so be it.

Even though the Communist bloc countries expelled Yugoslavia from the Soviet sphere, Tito nonetheless considered himself first and foremost a Communist. Ideologically, he distrusted the capitalist world, but now he was an outcast from the Communist one. Consequently, to survive, he had to open trade with the West. He also accepted military and financial aid from Western countries hoping to profit from the split.

Between 1945 and 1990, the Yugoslav economy lurched from one crisis to the next, but it was still better off than its Communist neighbors. Brief periods of economic growth between crises allowed Yugoslavs, in general, to prosper. There were, however, regional disparities that created arbitrary economic borders. Slovenia and Croatia were the richest areas, whereas Kosovo and Macedonia were the poorest. Serbia fell somewhere in the middle.[46] These arbitrary economic borders strengthened existing arbitrary social and cultural borders.

Despite fluctuations in the economy, Yugoslavs view the years between 1945 and 1966 as "golden years." Not that it was a particularly happy time, but the majority of the population experienced uniform levels of peace and prosperity. It was a period of reform and reaction, but generally there was surface calm. Although important debates within the party tended to split along nationalist lines, overall, the notion of "socialist Yugoslav patriotism" was greater than nationalist interests.

In 1966, however, arbitrary divisions once again began to unravel Yugoslav unity. It all began over issues of further decentralization and greater autonomy for the republics. Generally, Slovenia and Croatia, the richest republics, favored decentralization and more autonomy, because they could hold onto a larger portion of their incomes, rather than sending it to the state. By contrast, the poorer regions wanted centralization, because they benefited from these funds.

Until 1966, Aleksander Ranković, Yugoslavia's vice president and Tito's heir apparent, strongly supported central state control of the economy. Ranković, a Serb and a hard-line Communist, might have seen centralism as benefiting the Serbs. In any event, the party became deadlocked over this issue, and Tito had to intervene. He supported decentralization, which marked the beginning of the end for Ranković, who fell out of favor with Tito. In 1966, Ranković was forced to retire. Historians mark Ranković's fall as the beginning of true decentralization and liberalism unheard of before in a Communist country. It also, however, marks the beginning of a resurgence of Yugoslav separatism that would erupt in violence 20 years later.

The first blow against Yugoslav unity came in 1967 from a group of Croat intellectuals who initiated a movement to purify the Croatian language of all Serb words. Within three years, this seemingly innocuous issue expanded into a highly popular, highly political nationalist movement. Newspapers published columns to help people purge Serb words from everyday speech.[47] Then, questions arose over Croatia's constitution and what role the Serbs should play in it. Finally, some intellectuals started pushing for Croatian independence from Yugoslavia.

After hesitating for some months, Tito finally responded. In July 1971, he declared, "Under the cover of national interest all Hell is assembling. . . . In some villages Serbs, out of fear, are drilling and arming themselves. . . . Do we want to have 1941 again?"[48] Later that year, with the help of the conservative wing of the League of Communists of Yugoslavia, Tito crushed the nationalist movement in Croatia by purging and imprisoning thousands of Croats. He repeated this performance the following year in Serbia, where reformist democrats tried to implement liberal reforms. Tito's actions drove nationalist feelings underground but did not eradicate them. They were to surface again with a bloody vengeance in the 1990s.

Throughout the 1970s, nationalist sentiments also started to emerge in Kosovo and Bosnia. In Kosovo, Albanians began to take more control of the province. Increasing tensions between Serbs and Albanians dominated the political landscape. In 1979, Tito arrested hundreds of ethnic Albanians for being separatists. Then, in 1981, a round of violent rioting erupted, as Albanians sought to drive Serbs out of Kosovo. It took the army, commandos, and special police units to subdue the riots. Albanians defiled Orthodox churches and graveyards, causing great numbers of Serbs to leave the area. Rumors of rapes and murders of Serbs fanned the flames of nationalistic hatreds. Slowly, old historical borders reemerged to create much suffering once again.

This time, Tito was not there to bring the Yugoslav people back from the brink. In 1980, days before his eighty-eighth birthday, Tito died. Even if he had lived, it is doubtful that he could have preserved his Yugoslavia. Tito was the courageous leader of the Partisans, the uncompromising opponent of Stalin, and the driving force behind national equality and Yugoslav unity. His legacy, however, could not withstand the force of nationalism backed by centuries of strife. Yugoslavia was to once again be divided by artificial borders.

9

The End of Yugoslavia

When Tito died on May 4, 1980, he left no single successor to rule Yugoslavia. Rather, the Yugoslav Constitution provided for a complicated system involving a rotating federal presidency of eight members. The eight federal leaders adopted the slogan, "After Tito—Tito!" to imply that Communist unity rather than nationalist separatism would continue to be the underlying principle of Yugoslav governance. Everyone feared that, in the absence of Tito, arbitrary borders would tear the country apart yet again.

The feared transition from Tito's Yugoslavia to a collectively ruled federation seemed smooth initially. In the first few years after Tito's death, it appeared that Yugoslavia might remain unified and hold steady through the political and economic challenges ahead. Unfortunately, it was not to be. Within a decade, all eight members of Yugoslavia's collective leadership were ousted and replaced by a younger generation of leaders whose power was rooted in their native republics and whose nationalism began to strengthen the arbitrary borders between Yugoslav republics.

The plan for the evolution of the country from Tito's Yugoslavia to a collectively ruled federation was vague at best. It called for periodic rotation of political posts, including that of the president of Yugoslavia, among representatives of the republics. Earlier, in 1974, a new constitution had greatly decentralized Yugoslavia and transferred much power to the republics. Without a clear president to serve as the final arbiter, making decisions on pressing national economic and political issues ultimately became impossible. Republic and provincial leaders put local and ethnic interests above those of the country as a whole.

Yugoslavia's arbitrary borders began to unravel, as economic problems became crises. Throughout the 1970s, because Western credit was cheap and abundant, Yugoslavia borrowed heavily from Western countries. Yugoslav Communist economic planners, however, mismanaged the money. They invested in giant, extremely inefficient enterprises that satisfied political goals but were not economically sound. These enterprises, equipped with the latest technology, were poorly organized and operated. Their failure to yield expected profits produced an economic nightmare: By 1980, foreign debt increased by 400 percent.[49] Interest on the debt alone brought triple-digit inflation, as prices for food, clothing, and other necessities rose 60 percent every six months.[50]

Consequently, when a recession hit in the beginning of the 1980s, it devastated Yugoslavia's economy. Workers began to strike for higher wages and lower prices as hyperinflation demoralized the population. In early 1988, annual inflation stood at 160 percent; in December 1989, the monthly inflation rate reached 64.3 percent, for an annual rate of 2,500 percent.[51] The crisis reached a peak in the summer of 1990, when the banks revealed that they could not cover their customers' deposits because there was not enough money in the federal reserve. For the general public, this signaled total economic collapse, and, for many, financial ruin. In Kosovo, the poorest and least-developed region in Yugoslavia, the economic crisis was particularly dire.

At the same time, the country faced a political crisis in Kosovo. Almost as soon as Tito died, sporadic acts of arson and terrorism flared up again in Kosovo between Serbs and Albanians, culminating with riots in 1981. Tensions that existed along artificial ethnic borders only increased over time. In 1985, a petition signed by more than 2,000 Serbs living in Kosovo claimed that Albanians were forcing them out of the region and that local authorities were doing nothing to protect the Serbs.[52] Albanians allegedly burned Serb peasants' crops, blinded their livestock, and killed their chickens and goats. The following year, an entire Serb village threatened to immigrate to Serbia en masse because of Albanian harassment. Later that year, 200 Serbs from Kosovo went to Belgrade to protest the lack of legal and police protection against Albanian assaults.

Fearing that the crisis in Kosovo would destabilize the entire Yugoslav federation, the country's leaders opted for moderation and caution. Indeed, aside from trying to place blame for the political and economic crisis in Kosovo, federal authorities did nothing to improve the situation.

Slobodan Milošević, who became the Serbian Communist party leader in 1986, used the crises to advance the cause of Serbian nationalism. By 1986, the Serbian people wanted a change, and Milošević responded. He and his allies used mass rallies and demonstrations to promote Serbian "rights" and to make bold promises of a Serb victory in the battle for Kosovo. Official television stations and newspapers promoted Milošević's public image and put forth his political agenda. His program had three basic components that guaranteed the hardening of ethnic and political borders: urging constitutional amendments to reassert Serb control over its provinces; warning Slovenia and Croatia not to hasten Yugoslavia's disintegration; and generating fear that Croatian and Bosnian Serbs would be in danger if they ended up living in lands cut off from Serbia.[53]

Early in 1989, Milošević introduced amendments to the Yugoslav Constitution that ended Kosovo's autonomy and reasserted Serb control in the province. These changes resulted in widespread discontent and rioting in Kosovo, in which 22 Albanians and 2 policemen were killed. Subsequent arrests of Albanians ran into the thousands. In February 1990, the Yugoslav army sent in tanks and troops to quell the protests. Ethnic borders had once again turned deadly.

Meanwhile, in 1989, Milošević became the president of the Republic of Serbia. He forestalled the public swearing-in ceremony until the following month, however, to June 28. On the six-hundredth anniversary of the Battle of Kosovo Polje, June 28, 1989, Milošević made a dramatic appearance at the site of the battle, to assume the position of president. Arriving in a helicopter, he addressed nearly a million chanting and cheering people, including all of Yugoslavia's top politicians, assembled on the battlefield. In his speech, he declared:

> Serbs in their history have never conquered or exploited others. Through two world wars, they have liberated themselves

and, when they could, they also helped others to liberate themselves. . . . The Kosovo heroism does not allow us to forget that, at one time, we were brave and dignified and one of

President Slobodan Milošević addresses Serbian supporters during his swearing-in ceremony on June 28, 1989. Behind Milošević is a sign commemorating the 600-hundred-year anniversary of the Battle of Kosovo Polje, which many Serbs believe changed their nation's destiny.

the few who went into battle undefeated. . . . Six centuries later, again we are in battles and quarrels. They are not armed battles, though such things should not be excluded yet.[54]

The arbitrary borders of Yugoslavia were beginning to unravel. At the same time, revolutionary changes were sweeping central Europe. In the Soviet Union, Mikhail Gorbachev implemented political and economic restructuring that ended Russia's tight control over central Europe's Communist governments. As a result, Communist regimes throughout most of central Europe rapidly collapsed. In November 1989, the Berlin Wall, which had acted as an arbitrary border between the Communist and non-Communist world, was taken down. In Yugoslavia, the end of Communism incited nationalism to merge with democracy in a deadly way.

Traditionally, Yugoslavia straddled the border between East and West. Old arbitrary borders were recalled, and Catholic Croats and Slovenes saw a chance to disassociate themselves from Communist Yugoslavia. Their aim was to become a part of the western European community, as they had been under Habsburg rule. This goal took on a new sense of urgency in light of the "velvet" revolutions of 1989.

Unfortunately, by 1990, extremists on all sides began to dictate the course of events. Even as Albanians in Kosovo agitated for freedom from Serb domination, Croats and Slovenes made plans to declare independence. In Serbia, the media warned that if Croatia and Slovenia were allowed to leave Yugoslavia, the horrors of World War II would return. Milošević insisted that Serbia could not and would not allow the breakup of Yugoslavia.

In Croatia, the media increasingly depicted Serbs as terrorists. The police began searching and arresting Serbs, as relations between the two groups deteriorated. As police harassment intensified, several thousand Serbs fled northern Croatia, while several thousand more took refuge in a federal army compound. Serbian extremists sent volunteer troops with weapons to "help" their comrades. In one incident, an attempt by Croatian police to disarm a Serb enclave resulted in violence that left 12 Croats dead and 22 wounded.[55]

Once again, war erupted in Yugoslavia. This time the enemy came from within: a Yugoslavia divided by nationalistic hatreds that gathered along arbitrary ethnic borders. Yugoslavia would not survive it. War broke out in full force in Slovenia in June 1991, after Slovenia declared independence. Within 10 days, Slovenian territorial forces defeated the Yugoslav People's Army (JNA), leaving only nine civilians dead. By midsummer, war engulfed Croatia.

Croatia, like Slovenia, had declared independence. Unlike Slovenia, however, Croatia had a significant Serb population. Milošević announced that if Croatia left Yugoslavia, then the Serb-dominated areas of Croatia would leave Croatia. The ensuing war was much more devastating and lasted much longer than the war in Slovenia. The Serbs carried out programs of ethnic cleansing in Serb-dominated areas of Croatia. They also relied on heavy weapons to attack urban areas, causing much death and destruction.

By November 1991, both the Croats and Milošević had had enough. Mutinies and desertions plagued the JNA. Croatia suffered tremendous loss of life and territory. Therefore, both sides became willing to listen to foreign entreaties to stop the war and agreed to sign a cease-fire agreement. The United Nations deployed peacekeeping forces and appointed Cyrus Vance, the former U.S. Secretary of State, to try to broker the peace. The so-called Vance plan, however, caused more problems that it solved. Nonetheless, it did stop the shooting for a period of time.

The cease-fire between Serbia and Croatia allowed the Serbs to turn their attention to a deteriorating situation in Bosnia-Herzegovina. In the spring of 1992, the JNA began digging in positions around Sarajevo, the capital of Bosnia. As in Croatia, Milošević declared that if Bosnia left Yugoslavia, Bosnia's Serbs would carve their own state out of Bosnia. This new state would then unite with Greater Serbia.

At the beginning of the war in Bosnia, world attention focused on the Serbs' merciless shelling of Sarajevo. Consequently, absolutely dreadful things took place in the countryside and in small towns, hidden from foreign journalists. Here, too, the Serbs began great waves of ethnic cleansing and crimes against humanity not seen in Europe since Hitler's concentration camps. The Serbs set up detention camps that served as killing centers, and began a reign of terror that included the butchering of civilians, mass rape and torture, and the complete destruction of Islamic cultural artifacts, from mosques to books. The Serbs drove hundreds of thousands of Muslims, as well as Serbs and Croats, from their homes. By November 1991, 1.5 million people, nearly one-third the population, were refugees.[56]

By the winter of 1992, the war abated somewhat and new arbitrary borders were established. The old Yugoslavia ceased to exist, and a new Serbia extended from the border of Romania, across Serbia, Bosnia, and Croatia all the way to the Adriatic Sea. It looked like Milošević and the Serbs in Bosnia and Croatia had won.

As is often the case in this part of the world, however, everything changed in an instant. Earlier in the war, the United Nations had set up a safe zone for Bosnian Muslim refugees in the town of Srebrenica in Bosnia. In the summer of 1995, the Bosnian Serb military leader decided to get "revenge" on "Turks," as he called them, by attacking this safe zone. The Serbs overran UN peacekeeping forces and rounded up thousands of Muslim men and boys caught trying to flee from Srebrenica. They drove the Muslims into the forest and killed them, dumping the bodies in mass graves. Somewhere between 7,000 and 8,000 Muslims perished in the slaughter.

A few weeks later, Croatian forces moved to reclaim the land they had lost to the Serbs. With breathtaking speed, they retook all the territories occupied by the Serbs during the war. About 170,000 Serbs fled Croatia, as the arbitrary borders of Serbia once again shrank. Now, nearly 600,000 Serbs sought refuge in Serbia.[57]

By November 1995, the major fighting was over. After NATO air strikes forced the Serbs to withdraw from Sarajevo and other areas of Bosnia, peace became a possibility. The Serbs agreed to peace talks at a U.S. Air Force base in Dayton, Ohio. In December 1995, a peace agreement was reached. Within weeks, tens of thousands of NATO and UN troops moved into Bosnia to enforce the peace.

With the end of the war in Bosnia came hope for Serbs living in Serbia. Four years of constant fighting coupled with tough international sanctions left Serbia in dire economic condition. Inflation gave way to hyperinflation. By January 1994, the monthly inflation rate reached a staggering 313,563,558 percent.[58] As goods disappeared from the shelves, Serbia's black market flourished. Criminals flaunted their new wealth, moved

THE DAYTON PEACE ACCORDS

The Yugoslav wars of 1991–1994, the bloodiest conflict in Europe since World War II, shattered Yugoslavia's arbitrary borders and left more than 200,000 people dead and millions homeless. The war ended with the Dayton Peace Accords, which were negotiated at Wright-Patterson Air Force Base in Dayton, Ohio, but signed in Paris, France, on December 14, 1995. The agreement redrew the artificial borders of Yugoslavia's republics and has been hailed as a triumph of American and European diplomacy. Bosnia-Herzegovina, Croatia, and the Federal Republic of Yugoslavia (Serbia) signed the accords as representatives from the United States, Britain, France, Germany, and Russia witnessed the signing.

By signing the accords, Bosnia-Herzegovina, Croatia, and Serbia agreed to fully respect the sovereign equality of each other and to settle disputes by peaceful means. The agreement also provided for free and fair elections, a withdrawal of all troops, and the repatriation of refugees. It also granted NATO and the UN authority to oversee the peace. It also established arbitrary national borders and divided Bosnia into the Muslim-Croat Federation and the Bosnian Serb Republic.

One of the most important provisions of the accords required the investigation and prosecution of war crimes and other violations of humanitarian to desirable neighborhoods, and gained political influence. Through rigged elections and propaganda, however, Milošević remained in control.

With Serbia in such a weak position, despite calm on the surface, conflict began brewing again in Kosovo. For years, the Kosovo Albanians had wanted to be free from Serb control. Some Albanian leaders in Kosovo decided it was time to take up arms against the weakened Serbs. Slowly, a guerrilla war led by the Kosovo Liberation Army began. To stop the insurgency, the Serbian police drove hundreds of thousands of Kosovo Albanians out of their homes and into the hills. Facing winter with no food or shelter, the Albanians appealed to the West for help. The Serbs, who have always seen Kosovo as sacred Serb territory, refused to allow the Albanians to return.

law. As a result of this, many Yugoslav political and military leaders, including Slobodan Milošević, were indicted by the International War Crimes Tribunal at the Hague. Milošević, who died in March 2006 while on trial at the Hague, was charged with the 1995 massacre of thousands of Muslim men at Srebrenica, Bosnia. He was also charged with genocide in Bosnia, as well as the murder, imprisonment, inhumane treatment, and execution of Croats and other non-Serb civilians in Croatia. Finally, he was charged with the systematic killings of men, women, and children in Kosovo. Though he died before the end of his trial—in June 2006—the Supreme Court of Serbia ruled that he had ordered the death of two political opponents.

The Dayton Peace Accords were another attempt in a centuries-old struggle to create borders that will foster peace rather than warfare. The grouping of peoples with vastly different historical, social, economic, and religious borders has inevitably ended in bloodshed in the Balkans. The Dayton Peace Accords, like other agreements before it, sought to establish political borders that parallel the imagined borders of the Yugoslav peoples—borders steeped in history and solidified through bloodshed.

In 1999, the Serbian paramilitary entered Kosovo to punish ethnic Albanians who had rebelled against Serbian rule. As a result, thousands were killed and thousands more fled Kosovo in search of refuge. In March 1999, NATO forces began bombing the Serbian forces and eventually forced them to withdraw from Kosovo. Pictured here are ethnic Albanians who are celebrating the arrival of NATO troops in the town of Gnjilane on June 13, 1999.

On March 24, 1999, NATO began bombing Serbia and Serb positions in Kosovo; 78 days later, Milošević capitulated and withdrew his forces. During those 78 days, NATO bombs killed several hundred civilians, while Serbian forces slaughtered many thousands more.

In the end, Serbia's stunning losses in Slovenia, Croatia, Bosnia, and Kosovo coupled with severe economic crises at home, eroded support for Milošević. Indeed, many have pinned the blame for the breakup of Yugoslavia on Milošević. Within a year after the NATO bombing in Kosovo, a wave of popular protests forced Milošević to grant new elections. He overwhelmingly lost the election but refused to step down as Serbia's president. On October 5, 2000, hundreds of thousands of people took to the streets, and a national strike was declared. Ten days later, protesters stormed the parliament and forced him to resign (In February 2002, Miloščvić was put on trial for committing war crimes and genocide for his actions during the Yugoslav and Kosovo wars. Shortly before the trial was set to conclude in 2006, Milošević died of a heart attack in March of that year.) Like Yugoslavia before it, the arbitrary borders of Milošević's empire crumbled.

The arbitrary borders that shaped the country of Yugoslavia were demolished with such thoroughness that the name itself has disappeared from the map. With the destruction of these borders, peace has returned to the Balkan Peninsula. In some areas of the former Yugoslavia, however, it is an uneasy peace. All the old ethnic, social, and religious borders still exist. Bosnia is preserved as a single state, but it is divided into two parts: 51 percent of the country's territory is made up of a Muslim-Croat Federation, whereas 49 percent belongs to a Serb republic. The Kosovo region of Serbia is under UN administration until decisions can be made about its future. Albanians in Kosovo long to become part of a greater Albania, whereas the Serbs favor a partition similar to that in Bosnia.

In the lands of the South Slavs, arbitrary borders have been sources of conflict for centuries. Whether imposed by foreign powers or created internally, these borders have been the fracture lines along which wars have raged. Elusive though it might seem at times, however, peace and security in the region is not impossible. The imaginary lines of historical fate that create these borders can be removed. Indeed, in 2002, the presidents of Serbia, Croatia, and Bosnia met for the first time since the Yugoslav wars and agreed to respect the status quo in the region. Since then, there have been increasing signs of cooperation to combat common problems. The artificial borders of geography, nationality, history, and religion do not have to be divisive. Whether the governments of the post-Yugoslav states can learn that lesson remains to be seen.

600 B.C. Greeks set up trading posts along the Adriatic coast.

300 B.C. Greeks establish colonies along the Adriatic coast.

200 B.C. Romans arrive on the Adriatic coast and begin to dominate from the Balkan Peninsula eastward.

A.D. 395 Roman Empire splits into Eastern (Byzantine) and Western (Roman) spheres.

700–800 Slavic tribes move onto the Balkan Peninsula and settle in the central region of the peninsula.

910–928 Byzantine and Roman authorities recognize Tomislav as the king of the first Croatian state.

1052 The Church splits into the Catholic Church, centered in Rome, and the Orthodox Church, centered in Constantinople.

1102 Croatia welcomes a Hungarian king, thus becoming part of Hungary.

1168–1196 Stefan Nemanja I establishes the first Serbian kingdom.

1331–1355 The Serbian kingdom reaches its height under Stefan Dusan.

1353–1391 The Bosnian kingdom reaches its peak under Stefan Tvrtko.

1371 Serbian nobles choose Knez (Prince) Lazar to be king in response to rising threats from the Ottoman Empire; Ottoman Turks launch a surprise attack against the Serbs, defeating them on a battlefield now called "The Serbs' Destruction."

1389 Serbia is defeated by the Ottoman Turks at the battle of Kosovo Polje, which leads to the destruction of the Serbian kingdom and Ottoman domination of the Balkan Peninsula for the next 500 years.

1450s Hungary establishes control over Bosnia.

1463 The Ottoman Army conquers Bosnia and wrestles it out from under Hungarian control.

1699 The Ottoman Empire loses territory on the Balkan Peninsula to Europe for the first time under the Treaty of Karlowitz; Slavonia and Croatia, together with other lands, go to Austria, whereas most of the Croatian coast passes to Venice—this treaty marks the beginning of Ottoman decline and makes the Habsburg Empire the dominant power in the region.

Antioch Community High School Library

1700s Steady decline of the Ottoman Empire makes life increasingly difficult for different nationalities in the Yugoslav lands.

1789–1807 Sultan Selim III tries to reform the Ottoman Empire; he is murdered by Janissaries.

1804 Serbs revolt against the Ottoman Empire for the first time.

1806 Karageorge (Black George) defeats the Ottoman Army and captures Belgrade.

1807 Karageorge signs a Serbian-Russian alliance and rejects the sultan's offer of autonomy for Serbia— rather, he chooses to continue fighting, with Russia's support, for full independence; Turks respond with horrifying slaughter of Serbs.

910–928
Tomislav becomes
king of the first
Croatian state

1389
Serbia defeated by
Ottoman Turks
at Kosovo Polje

1699
Ottoman Empire
loses territory
in the Balkans
to Europe
for the first
time

910

1804

1463
Ottoman Army
conquers Bosnia

1102
Croatia becomes
part of Hungary

1804
Serbs revolt against
the Ottoman Empire for first time

1814   A second Serbian revolt headed by Miloš Obrenović is successful; Obrenović rules an autonomous Serbia until 1842.

1860–70s   Joseph Strossmayer, a Catholic bishop, proposes establishment of a unified Yugoslav state, centered in Croatia.

1878   Treaty of Berlin further erodes Turkish control in the Balkans; Habsburg Empire occupies Bosnia-Herzegovina.

1881   Serbian Radical Party is founded by Nikola Pašić.

1890s   Conflicts between Serbs and Croats dominate the decade.

1903   Karageorgevic Dynasty comes to power in Serbia and promises to create a genuine parliamentary democracy.

1991
Slovenia and Croatia declare independence from Yugoslavia

1914
Archduke Franz Ferdinand assassinated

1980
Tito dies

2006
Slobodan Milošević dies

1860

2006

1941
Germany invades Yugoslavia

1860–70s
Joseph Strossmayer proposes unification of Yugoslavia

1999
Serbian forces withdraw from Kosovo

1904 The Croatian People's Peasant Party (CPPP) is formed by Stjepan and Ante Radić.

1905 The Serbian Independent Party forges a Serb-Croat coalition to foster ethnic cooperation.

1908 Habsburg Empire annexes Bosnia-Herzegovina.

1912 In an attempt to take over Kosovo, the Serbs slaughter 20,000 Kosovar Albanians; more than 100,000 Kosovar Albanians flee.

1912–1913 First Balkan War with Turkey against Serbia, Greece, Bulgaria, and Montenegro.

1913 Second Balkan War engages Bulgaria against Greece, Serbia, and Romania.

1914 Archduke Franz Ferdinand is assassinated in Sarajevo by Gavrilo Princip, triggering World War I.

1917 Declaration of Corfu determines that the Yugoslav lands will be unified in a state ruled from Belgrade under the Karageorgevic' Dynasty.

1918 The Kingdom of Serbs, Croats, and Slovenes is established.

1921 The first Yugoslav constitution, the Vidovdan Constitution, is passed.

1928 Stjepan Radić, the popular leader of the CPPP, is assassinated by a member of the Serb Radical Party.

1929 King Alexander suspends the Yugoslav Constitution and abolishes the parliament.

1931 King Alexander issues a new constitution, which greatly expands the king's power.

1934 King Alexander is assassinated by Croat and Macedonian extremists.

1939 Serbs and Croats sign an agreement to reorganize the federal structure of Yugoslavia.

1941 Germany invades Yugoslavia; the Croatian Ustasha sides with the Nazis; Serbian Partisans oppose the Nazis; Kosovo becomes part of Italian-controlled Albania; Germans invade the Soviet Union during Operation Barbarossa.

1943 The wartime Partisan Parliament, known as the Anti-Fascist Council of the National Liberation of

Yugoslavia, or AVNOJ, meets in Bosnia and votes on a new Yugoslavia.

1947 Tito adopts a new Yugoslav constitution.

1948 Tito breaks with Stalin.

1966 Aleksander Ranković, Yugoslavia's vice president and Tito's heir, is forced to retire.

1967 A group of Croat intellectuals starts a popular Croatian nationalist movement.

1974 A new Yugoslav constitution greatly decentralizes the state.

1979 Hundreds of ethnic Albanians in Kosovo are arrested for being separatists.

1980 Tito dies.

1981 Violence erupts in Kosovo as Albanians seek to drive Serbs out of the region.

1986 Slobodan Milošević becomes leader of the Serbian Communist Party.

1989 Slobodan Milošević becomes president of the Republic of Serbia—a new Yugoslav constitution cancels Kosovo's autonomous status; violence again erupts throughout the region.

1991 Slovenia declares independence from Yugoslavia— after a 10-day war, Slovenia wins independence; Croatia declares independence from Yugoslavia, and war ensues.

1991–1994 War breaks out between Croatia and Milošević's Yugoslavia.

1992–1996 The Yugoslav People's Army (JNA) places Sarajevo under siege.

1995 Serbs slaughter thousands of Muslims at the UN safe zone at Srebrenica in Bosnia; Croatia retakes land lost earlier in the war to the Serbs; NATO air strikes force Serbs to retreat from Sarajevo; peace talks begin at Wright-Patterson Air Force Base in Dayton, Ohio; Dayton Peace Accords signed in Paris; Yugoslavia ceases to exist.

1996 Slobodan Milošević is indicted by the International War Crimes Tribunal at the Hague for crimes against humanity.

1998 Serbs begin to drive Albanians out of their homes in Kosovo and start a program of ethnic cleansing.

1999 NATO begins bombing Serbia and Serb positions in Kosovo; 78 days later, Milošević capitulates and withdraws his forces from Kosovo.

2000 Slobodan Milošević is forced to resign as president of Serbia.

2001–2006 Slobodan Milošević is on trial at the Hague for war crimes committed during the 1991–1994 Balkan wars; he dies in March 2006 of a heart attack.

2002 The presidents of Serbia, Croatia, and Bosnia meet for the first time since the Balkan wars and agree to respect the status quo in the region.

Chapter 1

1. Zlata Filipovic, *Zlata's Diary: A Child's Life in Sarajevo*. New York: Penguin Books, 1994, p. 1.
2. Ibid., pp. 62–63.
3. Ibid., pp. 135–136.
4. Laura Silber and Allen Little, *Yugoslavia: Death of a Nation*. New York: Penguin Books, 1997, p. 205.
5. Ibid., p. 252.

Chapter 2

6. Robert D. Kaplan, *Balkan Ghosts: A Journey Through History*. New York: Vintage Books, 1994, p. 31.
7. John R. Lampe, *Yugoslavia as History: Twice There Was a Country*. New York: Cambridge University Press, 1996, p. 23.
8. Ibid., p. 19.

Chapter 3

9. Barbara Jelavich, *History of the Balkans: Eighteenth and Nineteenth Centuries*. New York: Cambridge University Press, 1999, p. 89.

Chapter 4

10. Leslie Benson, *Yugoslavia: A Concise History*. New York: Palgrave, 2004, p. 6.

Chapter 5

11. Lampe, *Yugoslavia*, p. 70.
12. For discussion on the new imperialism in the Balkans, see L. S. Stavrianos, *The Balkans Since 1453*. New York: Holt, Rinehart, and Winston, 1958, pp. 414–417.
13. Ibid., p. 457.
14. Ibid., p. 460.
15. Ibid.
16. Ibid, p. 462.

Chapter 6

17. Leslie Benson, *Yugoslavia: A Concise History*. New York: Palgrave, 2004, p. 21.

18. Barbara Jelavich, *History of the Balkans: Twentieth Century*. New York: 1983, p. 145.
19. Ibid., p. 150.
20. Branka Prpa-Jovanović, "The Making of Yugoslavia," in Jasminka Udovički and James Ridgeway, eds., *Burn This House: The Making and Unmaking of Yugoslavia*. Durham, N.C.: Duke University Press, 1997, p. 49.
21. Ibid., p. 51.
22. Ibid., p. 50.
23. Ibid.
24. Ibid., p. 54.
25. Jelavich, *History of the Balkans: Twentieth Century*, p. 201.

Chapter 7

26. Tim Judah, *The Serbs: History, Myth and the Destruction of Yugoslavia*. New Haven, Conn.: Yale University Press, 1997, p. 117.
27. Lampe, *Yugoslavia as History*, p. 207.
28. As quoted in Judah, *The Serbs*, p. 125.
29. Benson, *Yugoslavia*, p. 77.
30. As quoted in Judah, *The Serbs*, p. 128.
31. Ibid., p. 131.
32. Ibid.
33. Lampe, *Yugoslavia as History*, p. 200.
34. Stavrianos, *The Balkans*, p. 772.
35. Judah, *The Serbs*, p. 118.
36. Ibid., p. 117.
37. Stavrianos, *The Balkans*, p. 774.
38. Judah, *The Serbs*, p. 120.

Chapter 8

39. As quoted in Stavrianos, *The Balkans*, p. 802.
40. Judah, *The Serbs*, p. 138.
41. Jelavich, *A History of the Balkans: Twentieth Century*. Cambridge: 1985, p. 272.
42. Ibid.
43. Lampe, *Yugoslavia as History*, p. 234.
44. Ibid, 235.
45. Jelavich, *A History of the Balkans*, p. 323.
46. Ibid., p. 323.
47. Ibid., p. 146.
48. As quoted in Ibid., p. 147.

49. Jasminka Udoviški and Ivan Torov, "The Interlude: 1980–1990," in Jasminka Udoviški and James Ridgeway, eds., *Burn This House*, p. 81.

Chapter 9

50. Ibid.
51. Benson, *Yugoslavia*, p. 152.
52. Ibid., p. 85.

53. Udoviški and Torov, "The Interlude," p. 88.
54. As quoted in Judah, *The Serbs*, p. 164.
55. Benson, *Yugoslavia*, p. 161.
56. Ibid., p. 166.
57. Jasmina Tesanovic, *Diary of a Political Idiot: Normal Life in Belgrade*. San Francisco: Midnight Editions, 2000, p. 14.
58. Ibid., p. 17.

PRIMARY SOURCES

Churchill, Winston. *The Second World War: Triumph and Tragedy*, Vol. 6. New York: Bantam, 1962.

Filipovic, Zlata. *Zlata's Diary: A Child's Life in Sarajevo*. New York: Penguin Books, 1994.

Tesanovic, Jasmina. *The Diary of a Political Idiot: Normal Life in Belgrade*. San Francisco: Midnight Editions, 2000.

Unfinished Peace: Report of the International Commission on the Balkans. Berlin: Carnegie Endowment for International Peace, 1996.

SECONDARY SOURCES

Benson, Leslie. *Yugoslavia: A Concise History*. New York: Palgrave, 2004.

Bianchini, Stefano, and George Schöpflin, eds. *State Building in the Balkans: Dilemmas on the Eve of the 21st Century*. Ravenna, Italy: Longo Editore, 1998.

Doder, Dusko, and Louise Branson. *Milošević: Portrait of a Tyrant*. New York: Simon and Schuster, 1999.

Dragnich, Alex N. "The Rise and Fall of Yugoslavia: The Omen of the Upsurge of Serbian Nationalism." *East European Quarterly* 23, no. 2 (June 1989): pp. 183–198.

———. *Yugoslavia's Disintegration and the Struggle for Truth*. New York: Columbia University Press, 1995.

Drakulic, Slavenka. *The Balkan Express: Fragments From the Other Side of War*. New York: W.W. Norton, 1993.

Ferfila, Bogomil. "Yugoslavia: Confederation of Disintegration?" *Problems of Communism* XL (July–August, 1991): pp. 18–30.

Glenny, Misha. *The Fall of Yugoslavia: The Third Balkan War*. New York: Penguin Books, 1996.

Held, Joseph, ed. *The Columbia History of Eastern Europe in the Twentieth Century*. New York: Columbia University Press, 1992.

Jelavich, Barbara. *History of the Balkans: Eighteenth and Nineteenth Centuries.* New York: Cambridge University Press, 1985.

———. *History of the Balkans: Twentieth Century.* New York: Cambridge University Press, 1985.

Judah, Tim. *The Serbs: History, Myth, and the Destruction of Yugoslavia.* New Haven, Conn.: Yale University Press, 1997.

Kaplan, Robert D. *Balkan Ghosts: A Journey Through History.* New York: Vintage Books, 1996.

Kumar, Radha. *Divide and Fall? Bosnia in the Annals of Partition.* London: Verso Press, 1999.

Lampe, John R. *Yugoslavia as History: Twice There Was a Country.* New York: Cambridge University Press, 1996.

———, and Mark Mazower, eds. *Ideologies and National Identities: The Case of Twentieth-Century Southeastern Europe.* Budapest: Central European University Press, 2004.

Oliver, Ian. *War and Peace in the Balkans: The Diplomacy of Conflict in the Former Yugoslavia.* London: I.B. Tauris, 2005.

Remet, Sabrina Petra. *Balkan Babel: The Disintegration of Yugoslavia From the Death of Tito to Ethnic War.* Boulder, Colo.: Westview Press, 1996.

Silber, Laura, and Allan Little. *Yugoslavia: Death of a Nation.* New York: Penguin Books, 1997.

Stavrianos, L. S. *The Balkans Since 1453.* New York: Holt, Rinehart, and Winston, 1958.

Stoianovich, Traian. *Balkan Worlds: The First and Last Europe.* Armonk, N.Y.: M.E. Sharpe, 1994.

Udovicki, Jasminka, and James Ridgeway, eds. *Burn This House: The Making and Unmaking of Yugoslavia.* Durham, N.C.: Duke University Press, 1997.

BOOKS

Mertus, Julie A. *Kosovo: How Myths and Truths Started a War.* Berkeley, Calif.: University of California Press, 1999.

Naimark, Norman M., and Holly Case, eds. *Yugoslavia and Its Historians: Understanding the Balkan Wars of the 1990s.* Palo Alto, Calif.: Stanford University Press, 2003.

Rogel, Carole. *The Breakup of Yugoslavia and the War in Bosnia.* Westport, Conn.: Greenwood Press, 1998.

Thomas, Raju G. C., ed. *Yugoslavia Unraveled: Sovereignty, Self-determination, Intervention.* New York: Lexington Books, 2003.

WEB SITES

BBC Yugoslavia 1918–2003
http://www.bbc.co.uk/history/state/nations/yugoslavia_01.shtml.

Twenty-five Lectures on Balkan History
http://www.lib.msu.edu/sowards/balkan.

The General Framework Agreement (The Dayton Accords)—NATO-IFOR
http://www.nato.int/ifor/gfa-home.htm.

International Criminal Tribunal for the Former Yugoslavia
http://www.un.org/icty/

page:

ii: © Infobase Publishing
 5: Associated Press, AP
12: Associated Press, AP
19: © Erich Lessing/Art Resource, NY
21: © Hulton Archive/Getty Images
28: © Infobase Publishing
36: © Infobase Publishing
41: © Hulton Archive/Getty Images
49: © Hulton Archive/Getty Images
55: © Hulton Archive/Getty Images

60: © Infobase Publishing
61: © Infobase Publishing
68: © Hulton Archive/Getty Images
74: © Hulton Archive/Getty Images
83: Associated Press, AP
86: Associated Press, AP
94: © Time & Life Pictures/Getty Images
100: © Infobase Publishing
108: © Reuters
114: Associated Press, AP

Cover: © University of Texas at Austin

Kate Transchel is professor of history at California State University, Chico. Specializing in Russia and the Balkans, she has published more than a dozen articles and encyclopedia entries on the history and culture of the Soviet Union. Her most recent book, *Under the Influence: Working-class Drinking, Temperance, and Cultural Revolution in Russia, 1895–1932*, was published in March 2006 by the University of Pittsburgh Press. During the 1990s, Transchel helped establish and served as chair of the nation-wide Coordinative Council on Alcoholism and Drug Addiction in Moscow, Russia. She also teaches cross-cultural communication and competency training on the history and culture of the Balkans and Russia for various U.S. Department of Defense agencies.

George J. Mitchell served as chairman of the peace negotiations in Northern Ireland during the 1990s. Under his leadership, a historic accord, ending decades of conflict, was agreed to by the governments of Ireland and the United Kingdom and the political parties in Northern Ireland. In May 1998, the agreement was overwhelmingly endorsed by a referendum of the voters of Ireland, North and South. Senator Mitchell's leadership earned him worldwide praise and a Nobel Peace Prize nomi-nation. He accepted his appointment to the U.S. Senate in 1980. After leaving the Senate, Senator Mitchell joined the Washington, D.C. law firm of Piper Rudnick, where he now practices law. Senator Mitchell's life and career have embodied a deep commitment to public service and he con-tinues to be active in worldwide peace and disarmament efforts.

James I. Matray is professor and chair of the History Department at California State University, Chico. He has published more than 40 articles and book chapters on U.S.–Korean relations during and after World War II. Author of *The Reluctant Crusade: American Foreign Policy in Korea, 1941–1950* and *Japan's Emergence as a Global Power*, his most recent pub-lication is *East Asia and the United States: An Encyclopledia of Relations Since 1784*. Matray also is international columnist for the *Donga Ilbo* in South Korea.